D0810315

The Great American Christmas Book

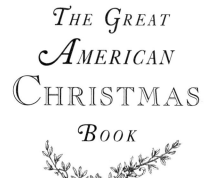

THE GREAT
AMERICAN
CHRISTMAS
BOOK

THE OVERLOOK PRESS
Woodstock & New York

This edition first published in the United States in 2007 by
The Overlook Press, Peter Mayer Publishers, Inc.
Woodstock & New York

WOODSTOCK:
One Overlook Drive
Woodstock, NY 12498
www.overlookpress.com
[for individual orders, bulk and special sales, contact our Woodstock office]

NEW YORK:
141 Wooster Street
New York, NY 10012

Copyright © 2007 by The Overlook Press

All rights reserved. No part of this publication may be reproduced
or transmitted in any form or by any means, electronic or
mechanical, including photocopy, recording, or any information
storage and retrieval system now known or to be invented,
without permission in writing from the publisher,
except by a reviewer who wishes to quote brief passages
in connection with a review written for inclusion in a magazine,
newspaper, or broadcast.

Cataloging-in-Publication Data is available from the Library of Congress

Compiled and edited by Aaron Schlechter
Original material by Marina R. Zhavoronkova and Ariel Berkower
Binding design by Ottessa Moshfegh
Book design and type formatting by Bernard Schleifer
Manufactured in the United States of America
ISBN-13 978-1-58567-982-9
10 9 8 7 6 5 4 3 2 1

Contents

CHRISTMAS FESTIVITIES AND HOME-MADE GIFTS

*A*MONG all the days we celebrate Christmas stands first and foremost in our thoughts, the holiday of holidays. Coming in the season of frost and snow it brings a cheering warmth to our hearts that defies the icy atmosphere, and the feeling of kindliness and good will toward everyone, which it awakens, seems in response to the words the angels sang on our first Christmas, "On earth peace, good will toward men."

Christmas is not merely a day set apart for feasting, giving and receiving presents, and for merrymaking. The day on which we celebrate the birth of our Lord is a time of rejoicing for rich and poor alike, and Christmas is Christmas still, although we may receive and can offer no presents and our feast is humble indeed.

Feeling this, let us keep the Christmas festival as it should be kept, right happily and merrily. Let us decorate our homes to the best of our ability in honor of the day, and supply all deficiencies with happy hears and smiling faces.

A friend of the writer's once remarked, as she busied herself with some Christmas-cards she was preparing to send to the hospitals, "I always like to tie a sprig of evergreen on each card; it looks and smells so Christmasy." And so it does. Even few pieces of evergreen, tacked over doorways or branching out from behind picture-frames, give a room a festive, Christmaslike appearance that nothing else can, and as evergreens are so plentiful here in America there are few houses that need be without their Christmas decorations. Holly, too, with its brilliant red berries peeping cheerily forth from their shelter of prickly leaves, adds brightness to the other adornments, and when the white-berried mistletoe can also be obtained all the time-honored materials for the Christmas decorations are supplies.

Though we are Americans, our ancestors came from many nations, and we have therefore a right and claim to any custom we may admire in other countries. We may take our Christmas celebrations from any people who observe the day and combining many, evolve a celebration which in its variety will be truly American.

From Germany we have already taken our Christmas-tree; from Belgium our Christmas-stocking; Santa Claus hails from Holland, and old England sends us the cheery greeting, Merry Christmas!

The custom the French children have of arranging their shoes on the hearth-stone on Christmas-Eve for the Christ-child to fill with toys or sweetmeats, is too much like our own Christmas stocking to offer any novelty. The Presepio, or Holy Manger, of the Roman Catholic countries, which represents the Holy Family at Bethlehem, with small wooden or was figures for the characters, is more suitable for the church celebration, but in Sweden and Denmark they have a peculiar method of delivering their Christmas-presents which we might adopt to our advantage, for it would be great fun to present some of our gifts in their novel manner.

Instead of describing this custom we will tell you just how to carry it out and will call it the

JULKLAPP,

which in Denmark and Sweden means Christmas-box or gift.

Before Christmas-Day arrives all the presents intended for the Julklapp delivery must be prepared by enclosing them in a great many wrappings of various kinds, none of which should in any way suggest their contents.

If one of the presents is a pretty trinket, wrap it up in a fringed tissue paper, such as is used for motto candy or sugar-kisses; place it in a small box, and tie the box with narrow ribbon; then do it up in common, rough brown paper, and wrap the package with strips of cloth until it is round like a ball; cover the ball with a thin layer of dough, and brown in the oven. Pin it up in a napkin, wrap in white wrapping paper and tie with a pink string.

The more incongruous the coverings, the more suitable they are for the Julklapp. You may enclose other gifts in bundles of hay, rolls of cotton or wool, and use your own pleasure in choosing the inner wrappings. It will be the wisest plan to always use something soft for the outside covering, the reason of which you will understand when the manner of delivery is explained. Each package must be labeled with the name of the person for whom it is intended, and if an appropriate verse, epigram, or proverb be added it will be the cause of fresh mirth and laughter.

The Julklapp delivery may, and probably will commence very early Christmas morning, for the little folks, always early risers on this day, will no doubt be up be-times, and ready for the business of the day. The first intimation the less enterprising members of the family will have that Christmas has dawned, will be a loud bang at the chamber door, followed by a thump of something falling on the bed or the sleeper's chest. Then springing up and opening startled eyes, from which all sleep has been thus rudely banished, one will probably discover a large bundle of *something* on the bed or lying on the floor close beside it. It will be useless to rush to the door to find from whom or where this thing has come, for although a suppressed giggle may be heard outside the door just after feeling the thump, nothing will be met upon opening it, but dead silence, and nothing seen but the empty hall.

At any time during the day or evening the Julklapps may arrive and when all look toward the door, as a loud rap is heard, whizz! something comes through the window and lands in the middle of the room. A sharp tap at the window is followed by the opening and closing or a door, and a bundle of straw, wool, paper, or cloth, as the case may be, lands in someone's lap. In short the Julklapps may come from any and every direction, and when one is least expecting them, and so the surprises and excitement are made to last until, weary with the fun and gayety of the day, the tired merry-makers seek their beds on Christmas-night.

If it has not been made plain enough who, or what causes the mysterious arrivals of the Julklapps we will say that the whole household join in the conspiracy, and the packages come from the hands of each of its members. The

POLISH CUSTOM

of searching for Christmas gifts, which have previously been hidden in all manner of places in the house, is one the children will delight in, and one that, introduced at a Christmas party, will provoke no end of merriment and fun.

THE BRAN PIE

is an English dish, but is quite as well suited to the American taste. It is an excellent means of distributing trifling gifts and may be new to some of you.

Use a large, deep brown dish for the pie. Put in it a gift for everyone who will be at the Christmas dinner, and cover them over thickly with bran, ornament the top by sticking a sprig of holly in the center. After dinner have the bran pie put on the table with a spoon and plates beside it, and invite everyone to help her or himself, each spoonful bringing out whatever it touches. Comical little articles may be put in the pie, and the frequent inappropriateness of the gift to the receiver of it, helps to create laughter.

The Bran Pie should be the secret of not more than two persons, for, like all thing pertaining to Christmas gifts, the greater the surprise, the more pleasure there will be in it.

THE BLIND MAN'S STOCKING

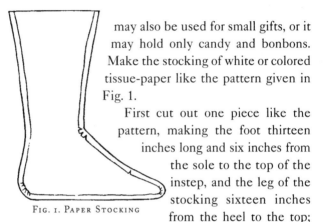

may also be used for small gifts, or it may hold only candy and bonbons. Make the stocking of white or colored tissue-paper like the pattern given in Fig. 1.

First cut out one piece like the pattern, making the foot thirteen inches long and six inches from the sole to the top of the instep, and the leg of the stocking sixteen inches from the heel to the top;

FIG. I. PAPER STOCKING

then cut another, one inch larger all around than the first. Place the two together fold the edge of the larger over the smaller piece and paste it down all around except at the top. Fill the stocking with small gifts or sweetmeats, tie a string around the top to keep it fast, and suspend it from the center of a doorway. Blindfold each player in turn, put a long, light stick in her hand, a bamboo cane will do, and lead her up within reach of the stocking and tell her to strike it. When anyone succeeds in striking the stocking and a hole is torn in it, the gifts or candy will scatter all over the floor to be scrambled for by all the players. Each player should be allowed three trials at striking the stocking.

Young children are always delighted with this Christmas custom, and the older ones by no means refuse to join in the sport.

Home-made Gifts

That the children may do their share toward filling the Christmas stockings, adding to the fruit of the Christmas tree, helping with the Julklapps, contributing to the Bran Pie or Blind Man's Stocking, we give these hints on home-made Christmas gifts, all of which are inexpensive and easily constructed.

Chamois for Eye-glasses

Cut out two circular pieces of chamois-skin about the size of a silver half-dollar, bind the edges with narrow ribbon, and fasten the two pieces together with a bow of the same. Print with a lead pencil on one piece of the chamois-skin, "I Make all Things Clear," and go over the lettering with a pen and India ink, or you may paint the letters in colors to match the ribbon. Fig. 2 shows how it should look when finished.

Fig. 2. Chamois for Eye-glasses

GLOVE PEN-WIPER

Cut four pieces from thin, soft chamois-skin, like the outline of Fig. 3. Stitch one with silk on the sewing-machine, according to the dotted lines. Cut two slits at the wrist through all the pieces as shown in Fig. 3, and join them together by a narrow ribbon passed through the openings, and tied in a pretty bow, Fig. 4.

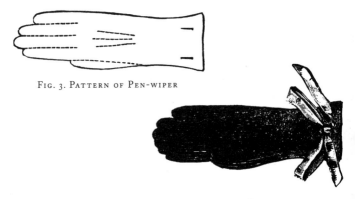

FIG. 3. PATTERN OF PEN-WIPER

FIG. 4. PEN-WIPER

SACHET

Open out an envelope, and cover it with white or cream-colored silk, refold carefully, joining the edges with stiff mucilage, using as little as possible. In place of a letter enclose a layer of cotton sprinkled with sachet-powder, fasten the envelope with sealing-wax as in an ordinary letter. Address it with pen and ink, to the one for whom it is intended. Print on it, like a stamp,

"Christmas, December 25," and fasten a cancelled stamp, taken from an old letter, on one corner. The finished sachet is shown in Fig. 5.

FIG. 5. SACHET

A BOOK-MARK

Cut out the corner of a full-sized, linen-lined envelope, making the piece four inches long, and one and a half inches wide. Write on one side with pen and ink, or paint the lettering in color, "A Fresh Mind Keeps the Body Fresh." The book-mark will fit over the book-leaf like a cap, and is excellent for keeping the place. Fig. 6

FIG. 6. BOOK-MARK

A SCRAP-BAG

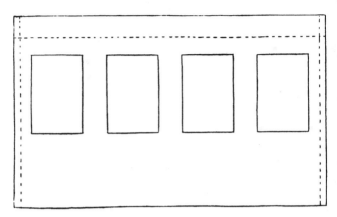

FIG. 7. PATTERN OF SCRAP-BAG

Scrap-bags have been fashioned in many shapes and sizes, and of all sorts of material, still it remains to be shown in what manner Christmas cards may add in decoration and beauty to these useful articles. From your collection choose four cards of the same size, then on a piece of bright silk or cloth sew the cards at equal distances apart, as in Fig. 7, stitching them around the edges on the sewing machine. At the dotted line fold over the top of the bag as if for a hem, making the narrow fold lap just cover the upper edge of the card; stitch this down to form a binding.

FIG. 8 SCRAP-BAG

After joining the bag at the dotted lines on the sides, gather the bottom up tight and fasten to it a good-sized tassel; then sew on each side a heavy cord with tassels placed where the cord joins the bag, as seen in Fig 8. The cord and tassels of the example were made of scarlet worsted.

A Walnut-shell Turtle

For an ornament to be used on a pen-wiper, or simply as a pretty toy, the little turtle is appropriate. It is made of half an English walnut, which forms the turtle's back or shell, glued on a piece of card-board cut after the diagram given in Fig. 9. Paint the card-board as nearly as possible the color of the shell, and the eyes black. When perfectly dry glue the shell securely to the card-board, bend down and out the feet a little, in order to make the turtle stand; bend the head up, and the tail down, as in Fig. 10.

Fig. 9 Pattern of Turtle

Fig. 10. Turtle

Here are some home-made toys which the children can make to give to one another.

Miss Nancy

Miss Nancy (Fig. 13) is fashioned from a piece of pith taken out of a dried cornstalk. Cut away the stalk until the pith is reached; then take a piece of the pith, about six inches long and whittle out one end to resemble a head as in Fig. 11, draw a face on the head with pen and ink, and glue half of a lead bullet on the lower end of the pith (Fig. 12). Make Miss Nancy's costume

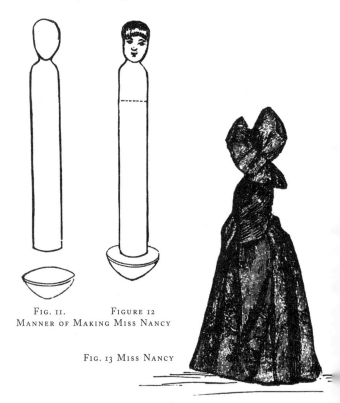

Fig. 11.   Figure 12
Manner of Making Miss Nancy

Fig. 13 Miss Nancy

of a skirt, composed of some bright-colored Japanese paper, a shawl made of a piece of soft ribbon or silk, and a cap of white swiss. The peculiarity of the little lady is that she insists upon always standing upright, no matter in what position she is placed.

A Soft Ball

A very pretty and safe return ball for the little ones to play with may be made of paper (Fig. 14), which, being soft, precludes all danger of "thumps and bumps."

Take a piece of newspaper, and, using both hands, roll it and fold it into something of the required shape. Then place it in the center of a square piece of bright-colored tissue paper; take the four corners of the tissue-paper up to the center of the top of the ball, fold them over, also fold and smooth down what fullness there may be; next place a small round piece of gold, silver, or some contrasting colored paper on the top of the ball, making six or eight divisions; tie a piece of elastic to the string where it crosses on the top of the ball, then past over this a small artificial flower. In the other end of the elastic, make a loop to fit over the finger, or tie on it a small brass ring.

Fig. 14. Paper ball

If a tiny sleigh-bell be placed in the center when the ball is being made, it will give a cheerful little tinkling noise whenever the ball is thrown.

A LIVELY ROOSTER

To make the rooster (Fig. 15), cut out of stiff cardboard Figs. 16, 17, 18, and 19. Tie on Figs. 16 and 17 each a piece of string seven and one-half inches long. Then attach the head and tail to the body by running a string through holes at A in Fig. 17 and A in Fig. 18, and another through B in Fig. 16 and B in Fig. 18. Bring the head and tail up close to the body and fasten the ends of the strings down securely with court-plaster or pieces of paper pasted over them. Bend Fig. 18 at dotted line C; then on the space marked E, paste the portion of Fig. 19 marked E after bending it at dotted line O. Again bend Fig. 19 in the same direction at dotted line P, and paste it across the space marked P, on Fig. 18. When all is fastened together, and the paste perfectly dry, paint the rooster to look as life-like as possible. Tie the strings of Figs. 16 and 17 together four inches from where they are fastened on, then again about three inches lower down, and attach a weight to the ends. A common wooden top, with a tack in the head (Fig. 20), will answer the purpose nicely. To bring the rooster to life, place him on the mantel-piece, with a book serving as a weight on the projection of Fig. 19, swing the top and he will move his head and tail in the most amusing manner.

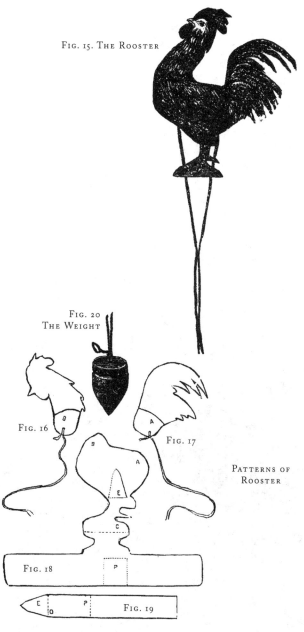

FIG. 15. THE ROOSTER

FIG. 20
THE WEIGHT

FIG. 16

FIG. 17

PATTERNS OF
ROOSTER

FIG. 18

FIG. 19

FAIRY DANCERS

Among the gifts made by little hands, a box, containing a set of fairy dancers, will be a most novel and welcome addition. These little figures, when placed on the piano, will move as soon as the keys are touched, dancing fast or slow in perfect time to the music. They may all be made to resemble fairies as in Fig. 21, or a famous collection of figures in the costumes of different periods in history will be equally

FAIRY DANCERS

FIG. 21 A FAIRY DANCER   FIG. 22 PATTERN OF
                                        FAIRY DANCER

pretty and perhaps more interesting. Ladies in kirtles
and tunics, gentlemen in slashed doublet and hose of
the Tudor times, Queen Elizabeth's starched ruffs
and farthingales, etc. All these dresses can be more
easily copied from pictures of the period than from
any written description of them. The materials used
for the costume must be of the lightest kind, for a
heavy dress will weigh down the dancer and hamper
its movements. To make the fairy (Fig. 21) trace Fig.
22 on cardboard and cut it out, sew a piece of bonnet-

wire down the back, as shown in diagram. Mark the slippers on the feet with ink or black paint, select a Christmas or advertising card representing a child, with a head of a suitable size, cut the head out and paste it on the fairy.

Gather two short skirts of tarlatan, make a waist of the same, sew with a few stitches to the doll, and cover the stitches with a sash of bright colored tissue paper; add a strip of tarlatan for a floating scarf, gluing it to the uplifted hands. Bend back the piece of cardboard projecting from the foot, and glue to it a small piece of bristle brush. The wire in the doll should belong enough to pass tightly around the brush, thus making it more secure.

BUTTERFLIES

Butterflies of brilliant hues, all hovering and circling, may take the place of the fairies, or they may mingle with them in the dance, presenting a scene indeed fairy-like. To make a butterfly, trace the pattern given in Fig. 23, on brilliantly colored paper. Form a body by rolling a small piece of beeswax between the fingers until it assumes the desired shape (Fig. 24); then attach the wings to the boy by softening the wax and sticking them to it. Wax a piece of black thread to stiffen it, and make a knot in each end (Fig. 25), bend this in the middle and stick it on to the head to form the antennae (Fig. 26). Fasten one end of a very fine wire securely in the middle of the wax body, and wrap the other end around a small piece of brush as seen in Fig. 27. A number of these butterflies placed on the pianoforte will move, bend and sway with the music as if endowed with life.

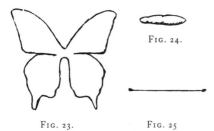

Fig. 24.

Fig. 23.   Fig. 25

Butterfly Pattern

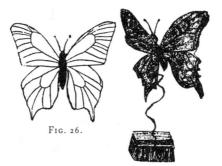

Fig. 26.

Fig. 27. Butterfly

Toys, also, which are small and light enough, can be made to "trip the light fantastic" in time to the music.

Select those most suitable and glue them to pieces of brush in the way described for thither dancers.

The children, generous little souls, always long to do their part towards making Christmas presents, and we hope that the suggestion we have offered will help them to manufacture, without other aid, many little gifts which their friends will prize the more highly for having been made by the loving little hands.

AMUSEMENTS AND GAMES
FOR THE HOLIDAYS

*W*INTER passed in-doors would be irksome indeed for a healthy, hearty child, and even the most delicate are the better for an outing now and then. The keen northwest wind, the biting frosts, the crisp atmosphere and the glistening ice and snow are not without their attractions, and we hope that no American child will neglect the opportunities this time of the year affords for healthy, enjoyable out-door pastime. It is well to follow the example of our Canadian siblings, and, clad in garments warm and appropriate, indulge in coasting, tobogganing, skating, sleighing, and walking.

The country, wrapped in its winter mantle, is very attractive. Many of our small animals and birds that city people are apt to associate only with a summer landscape, are to be found abroad in mid-winter, and upon a bright sunny day the birds are not only to be seen, but heard twittering and even singing in the hedges; they do not feel the cold and are enjoying themselves heartily. The reason the birds and wild creatures are so comfortably content, is because they are prepared for the weather, their clothing is not only soft and warm, but fits them perfectly, without interfering with their movements. Take a lesson from them, dress as becomingly as you choose, the birds always do that, but do not wear thin-soled shoes or anything that is uncomfortable; wrap up warm and you can enjoy yourself out of doors in the coldest weather just as well as the birds. The cold winds will only bring the roses to your cheeks, and the keen, invigorating air, health and suppleness to your body.

We do not think any person ever learned to skate, or coast, from reading the directions that can be given in a book. It is for that reason we have no chapter devoted to these sports and not because we do not believe in, and enjoy them, too. Therefore we will direct our attention to indoor sports, for they can be learned in this way and are quite as important as the others in filling out the list of winter amusements.

There are a great many days in winter when it is so stormy and disagreeable out-doors, one is glad enough to have the shelter of a roof and the warmth of a fire; these are the days and evenings when in-doors games are in demand, and during the holiday season, when work has been put aside, and you have nothing to do but enjoy yourself, any new diversion is always welcome. It is here then that we will insert the

New Game of Bubble Bowling

When the game of Bubble Bowling was played for the first time, it furnished an evening's entertainment, not only for the children, but for grown people also; even a well known general and his staff, who graced the occasion with their presence, joined in the sport, and seemed to enjoy it equally with their youthful competitors. Loud was the chorus of "Bravo!" and merry the laugh of exultation when the pretty crystal ball passed safely through its goal; and sympathy was freely expressed in many an "Oh!" and "Too bad!" as the wayward bubble rolled gaily off toward the floor, or, reaching the goal, dashed itself against one of the stakes and instantly vanished into thin air.

The game should be played upon a long, narrow table, made simply of a board about five feet long and eighteen inches wide, resting upon high wooden "horses." On top of the table, and at a distance of twelve inches from one end, should be fastened in an upright position, two stakes, twelve inches high; the space between the stakes should be eight inches, which will make each stand four inches from the nearest edge of the table. When finished, the table must be covered with some sort of woolen cloth; an old shawl or a breadth of colored flannel will answer the purpose excellently. Small holes must be cut at the right distance for the stakes to pass through. The cloth should be allowed to fall over the edge of the table, and must not be fastened down, as it will sometimes be necessary to remove it in order to let it dry.

BUBBLE BOWLING

It will be found more convenient, therefore, to use two covers, if they can be provided, as then there can always be a dry cloth ready to replace the one that has become too damp. The bubbles are apt to stick when they come upon wet spots, and the bowling can be carried on in a much more lively manner if the course is kept dry. Each of the stakes forming the goal should be wound with bright ribbons of contrasting colors, entwined from the bottom up, and ending in a bow at the top. This bow can be secured in place by driving a small brass-headed tack through the ribbon into the top of the stake. If the rough pine legs of the table seem too unsightly, they can easily be painted, or a curtain may be made of bright-colored cretonne—any other material will do as well, provided the colors are pleasing—and tacked around the edge of the table, so as to fall in folds to the floor. The illustration shows the top of the table, when ready for the game.

For an impromptu affair, a table can be made by placing a leaf of a dining-table across the backs of two chairs, and covering it with a shawl; lead pencils may be used for the stakes, and they can be held in an upright position by sticking them in the tubes of large spools, this sort of table the children can arrange themselves, and it answers the purpose very nicely. The other things to be provided for the game are a large bowl of strong soapsuds, made with hot water and common brown soap, and as many pipes as there are players.

The prizes for the winners of the game may consist of any trinkets or small articles that fancy or taste may suggest.

Bubble Bowling can be played in two ways. The first method requires an even number of players, and these must be divided into two equal parties. This is easily accomplished by selecting two children for captains, and allowing each captain to choose, alternately, a recruit for her party until the ranks are filled, or, in other words, until all the children have been chosen; then, ranked by age, or in any other manner preferred, they form in line on either side of the table. A pipe is given to each child, and they stand prepared for the contest. One of the captains first takes her place at the foot of the table, where she must remain while she is bowling, as a bubble passing between the stakes is not counted unless blown through the goal from the end of the table.

The bowl of soapsuds is place upon a small stand by the side of the bowling-table, and the next in rank to the captain, belonging to same party, dips her pipe into the suds and blows a bubble, not too large, which she then tosses upon the table in front of the captain, who, as first bowler, stands ready to blow the bubble on its course down through the goal. Three successive trials are allowed each player; the bubbles which break before the bowler has started them, are not counted.

The names of all the players, divided as they are into two parties, are written down on a slate or paper, and whenever a bubble is sent through the goal, a mark is set down opposite the name of the successful bowler.

When the captain has had her three trials, the captain on the other side becomes bowler, and the next in rank of her own party blows the bubbles for her. When this captain retires, the member of the opposite party, ranking next to the captain, takes the bowler's place and is assisted by the one whose name is next on the list of her own side; after her the player next to the captain on the other side; and so on until the last on the list has her turn, when the captain then becomes assistant and blows the bubbles.

The number of marks required for either side to win the game, must be decided by the number of players; if there are twenty—ten players on each side—thirty marks would be a good limit for the winning score.

When the game has been decided, a prize is given to that member of the winning party who has the greatest number of marks attached to her name showing that she has sent the bubble through the goal a greater number of times than any player on the same side. Or, if preferred, prizes may be given to every child belonging to the winning party. The other way in which Bubble Bowling may be played is simpler, and does not require an even number of players as no sides are formed.

Each bowler plays for themself, and is allowed five successive trials; if three bubbles out of the five be blown through the goal the player is entitled to a prize. The child acting as assistant becomes the next bowler, and so on until the last in turn becomes bowler, when the one who began the game takes the place of assistant.

When the evening lamps are lighted and the young folks, gathered cosily around the cheerful fire, begin to be at a loss how to amuse themselves, let them try the game of

BIOGRAPHICAL NONSENSE

A paper must be written by one of the players which will read like the following:

The name of a noted man.
A date between the flood and the present year.
The name of a noted man.

A country.
The name of some body of water or river.
Some kind of a vessel.
A country.
A country.
The name of a school.
A city.
A city, town, or country.
A city, town, or country.
A number.
The names of two books.
The name of one book.
A wonderful performance.
The name of a well-know person.
A profession or trade.
A term expressing the feeling entertained for another person.
A term descriptive of someone's appearance.
A word denoting size.
A term describing form.
A color.
A word denoting size.
The name of an article of some decided color.
The name of any article.
The name of any article.
A number of years.

This paper is to be passed to each member of the party who in turn will fill up the blanks left, with the words, terms, and names indicated.

When the blanks have been filled, one player must read the following, and another supply the words, when she pauses, from the paper just prepared, being sure to read them in their true order.

A BIOGRAPHY.

____ was born in ____ the same year when ____ discovered ____, by sailing through the ____ in a ____. His father was a native of ____; his mother of ____. He was educated at ____, in the city of ____. His first voyage, which was a long one, was from ____ to ____. He wrote three books before he was ____ years of age. They are ____, and ____. Her performed the miraculous feat of ____ with ____. He was a great ____, and one we shall ever ____. In appearance he was ____ being rather ____ of stature. His nose was ____, his eyes ____, his mouth ____, and hair the color of ____ adorned his head. He invariable carried in his hand a ____ and a ____, by which he was always known, and with which he is represented to this day. He died at the advanced age of ____.

The ridiculous combinations found in this game make it very funny.

COMICAL HISTORICAL TABLEAUX

are very amusing, and being impromptu require no preparation beforehand.

As in charades, the company must divide into two parties. But instead of acting as in charades, one party decides what event in history they will represent, and then they form a tableau to illustrate the event, making it as ridiculous as possible. The other party must try and guess what the tableau is; if they are successful, it is their turn to produce a tableau, if not, the first party must try another subject, and continue to do so until the subject of the tableau is correctly guessed.

We will give a few suggestions for the tableaux.

Balboa Discovering the Pacific Ocean

Place a pan of water on the floor in plain sight of the audience; then let someone dress up in a long cloak and high-crowned hat to impersonate Balboa, and stand on a table in the middle of the floor, while the rest of the performers, enveloped in shawls, crouch around. When the curtain is drawn aside, Balboa must be seen looking intently through one end of a tin horn, or one made of paper, at the pan of water.

Nero at the Burning of Rome

Nero, in brilliant robes made of shawls, sits on a table, surrounded by his courtiers, who are also in fantastic costumes. Nero is in the act of fiddling, his fiddle being a small fire shovel, and the bow a poker. On the floor in front of the group is placed a large shallow pan or tray, in which is set a small house, which has been hastily cut from paper. A lighted match is put to the paper house just as the curtains are parted. These two suggestions will no doubt be sufficient to show what the tableaux should be like and we need give no further illustrations.

Santa Hat Game

This is an ideal game to play during a holiday gathering while other festivities are taking place. Each guest wears a Santa hat and the only rule is that no one can remove their hat until the host does. As the day progresses, the host secretly removes his or her hat. As guests begin noticing, they slyly remove their own hats until there is only one Santa remaining.

LIVING CHRISTMAS CARDS

To impart seeming life to the little figures painted on the Christmas cards, is a performance intensely amusing to the little ones. A moving toy whose actions are life-like is always of great interest; but when a little flesh-and-blood head is seen nodding and twisting upon the shoulders of a figure painted on a card, the children fairly shout with delight.

Here is the method of bringing life into the bits of paste-board.

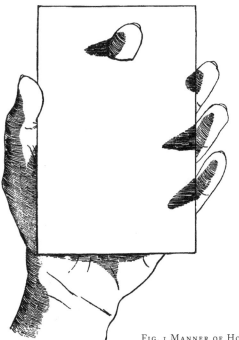

FIG. 1 MANNER OF HOLDING CARD

Fig. 2 Live Head with Peaked Cap

Select cards with pretty or comical figures, whose faces are the size of the ends of your first or second finger. Carefully cut the face out of a card; then with ink mark the features on your finger, and put it through the opening, as in Fig. 1. Place on this little live head a high peaked tissue-paper cap, and the effect will be exceedingly ludicrous (Fig. 2). A little Santa Claus who can really nod and bow to the children will be very amusing, and there are quite a number of Christmas cards which portray the funny, jolly little fellow.

Floral cards may have nodding fairies peeping out from among the petals of the flowers, whose heads are

FIG. 3. NODDING FAIRIES

crowned with queer little fairy caps, as in Fig. 3. If among your collection you have a card with a picture of a house on it, it will be amusing to thrust a little head wearing a night-cap, out of one of the window. Round holes will, of course, have to be cut in the cards wherever the heads are to appear.

Still another way of managing these living puppets is to cut in a piece of cardboard, five inches long and two inches wide, three round holes a little more than half an inch apart. Sew around the edge of the cardboard a gathered curtain of any soft material six inches deep. Sketch faces on three of your fingers, pass them under the curtain and through the holes in the cardboard. The curtain will fall around and conceal your hand, leaving the three heads appearing above (Fig. 4). on these heads place any kind of head-dress you choose, making them of paper; or caps of white swiss look quaint, and wee doll hats may be worn.

It is best to use a little mucilage or paste in fastening the hats on, that there may be no danger of their falling off with the movement of the fingers.

The hair may be inked, or little wigs made of cotton can be used.

If the little faces are painted with water colors, giving color to the cheeks and lips, the life-like appearance will be enhanced.

These little personages can be made to carry on absurd conversations, and a great deal of expression be given to the bobbing and turning of their heads. One person can easily manage the whole thing, and entertain a roomful with the performance of the living puppets.

Fig. 4 Living Puppets

HOW TO MAKE VARIOUS AND DIVERSE WHIRLIGIGS

WHO can watch machinery of any kind in motion, without experiencing an indefinable sort of pleasure? No matter how simple the contrivance may be, if it move it immediately interests us. This instinct, if I may so call it, that prompts us to watch and play with machinery is implanted in the brain of the lower animals as well as of man. I think no one can doubt that a kitten or a dog enjoys chasing a ball, and enters into the sport with as much zest as a college-boy does his game of football. It is this same indefinable desire for observing and experimenting with moving objects that prompts us to throw stones for the purpose of seeing them skip over the surface of the water, and to this instinct must be attributed the pleasure experienced by the school-boy with his

POTATO MILL,

which consists of simply a stick, a potato, a buckeye, or a horse-chestnut, and a string. The stick is whittled into the form shown in the illustration; a string is fastened to the stick about one-half inch below the knob on the top. The buckeye has a large hole bored through the middle, and a small hole bored through one side, to the middle hole; the string from the stick passes through the hole in the side of the buckeye; the end of the stick is sharpened and thrust into a potato.

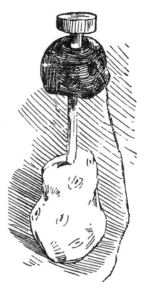

If the string be wound around the stick, and the buckeye held between the thumb and forefinger, the stick and potato may be made to spin rapidly by alternately pulling the string and allowing it to slacken; the motion imparted by the first pull continues long enough to wind the

THE POTATO MILL

string in the opposite direction, and thus, for an indefinite time, or until the string wears out by friction, the potato mill may be kept buzzing at a great rate.

Another machine the boys used to be very fond of was called

A SAW-MILL;

it was generally made out of the top of a tin can, with the rim knocked off and the edge cut into notches like a saw. Two strings passing through two holes near the center gave a revolving motion to the "buzzer" (Fig. 5 shows a saw-mill). By holding the strings so that the wheel hangs loosely in the middle, and swinging the wheel or "buzzer" around and around until the string becomes tightly twisted, the machine is wound up. As with the potato mill, the revolving motion is imparted

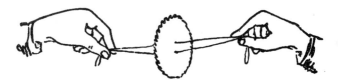

FIG. 5. A SAW MILL

by alternately puling and allowing the string to slacken, only in this case you must hold one end of the string in each hand (Fig. 5). When the boys can make a buzzer actually saw into a piece of board or shingle by allowing the edge of the wheel to strike the wood, the saw-mill is pronounced a success, and its value increased.

Very pretty and amusing toys may be made on the same principle as the saw or potato mills described. One of these little machines, a very fascinating one, is sold upon the streets of New York by the novelty peddlers. As the writer was passing along Broadway the other day, he saw an old acquaintance, known to almost all New Yorkers by the name of "Little Charlie." Little Charlie is not a small man, as his name might imply, but a large, good-natured, red-faced peddler, who stands all day long at the street corners. During the winter he sells small india-rubber dolls, crying out to the passers-by: "Well! Well! Well! Little Charlie! Double him up!" he doubles the little india-rubber dolls up in a comical manner to attract customers. The torrid summer heat is too much for the india-rubber dolls, and makes them sticky, so that they are laid aside during the hot weather, and Little Charlie, with the perspiration streaming from his face, no longer calls out in his accustomed manner, but stands silently twirling his summer novelty, trusting to the ever-changing colors of the toy to attract purchasers. One was bought that it might be introduced among the other whirligigs in this chapter.

THE RAINBOW WHIRLIGIG.

If you have a pair of dividers, make a circle upon a piece of card-board about two inches in diameter; inside this circle make six other circles (Fig. 6). A pair of scissors can be made to do the duty of a pair of dividers by spreading them apart the required distance and thrusting the points through a card to hold them in position (Fig. 7). Make a duplicate figure or disk and paint the parts of the inside circles, shaded in the diagram, different colors; for instance, A and D may be made blue, B and E green, C and F red. The points of the star in the center made by the intersection of the circumference of the circles should be painted the same color as the parts of the circle adjoining. Upon the second disk paint A and D blue, B and E yellow, C and F red.

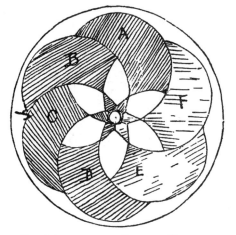

Fig. 6 A disk of the Rainbow Whirligig

FIG. 7 A PAIR OF
DIVIDERS

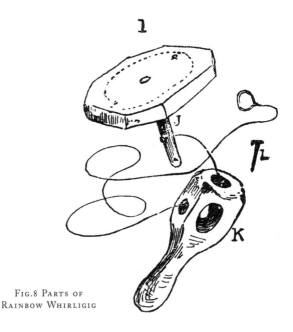

FIG.8 PARTS OF
RAINBOW WHIRLIGIG

Cut a piece of one-quarter inch pine into a square, with sides of about two and one-quarter inches in length; cut off the corners as shown by I, Fig. 8. In a hole in the center of I fasten tightly the round stick J. whittle out another piece for a handle K, and bore a hold through the top for the stick J to fin in loosely; bore another hold through one side for the string to pass through. In the illustration, as in the original from which the drawing was made, there is a large hole bored through two sides; but this is unnecessary, and only put in the diagram to better show the position of the string inside. Upon the wooden plate I, describe a circle about one and three-quarter inches in diameter. In the center of the two paper disks make holes large enough to fit with shoe-eyelets; then with tacks (L, Fig. 8) fasten the two paper disks on to the wooden plate at the points G and H, in such a manner that the tack passing through the eyelets will allow the disks to revolve freely. Attach a string to the stick J at a point that will come opposite the string-hole in the side of the handle, when the stick J is slid into the hole at the top of the handle K. the wooden disk is made to spin exactly in the same manner that motion is imparted to the potato mill already described. When in motion the colors on the paper disks will blend and produce, with each change of position, a number of beautiful variations. The two paper disks blend together, making a large circle three and one-half inches in diameter, composed of concentric rings of the most lovely hues—red, pink, purple, green, and all the different shades and combinations imaginable are portrayed with ever-changing variety by the spinning rainbow whirligig.

A PARADOXICAL WHIRLIGIG

is a very ingenious toy, consisting of a circle of white card-board, upon the surface of which any number of black rings are painted, one within the other, until it resembles an archery butt or target.

The disk is tacked or glued securely to a stick or handle (Fig. 9) so that it is impossible for it to really revolve, yet if you grasp the toy by the handle and give your arm a motion similar to that of the shaft of an engine, the disk upon the stick will appear to revolve like a wheel, and so closely does the optical delusion resemble actual motion that it will deceive almost any one who is not familiar with the experiment.

A picture of a wagon, with wheels made like the disks of the paradoxical whirligig, may be made, and the wheels will have all the appearance of revolving when a wabbling motion is imparted to the picture. There are many curious experiments that can be tried in this line—spirals may be made to twist around; pictured machinery may be given the appearance of actual moving wheels, etc. The philosophy of all this is best explained in the description of the next whirligig.

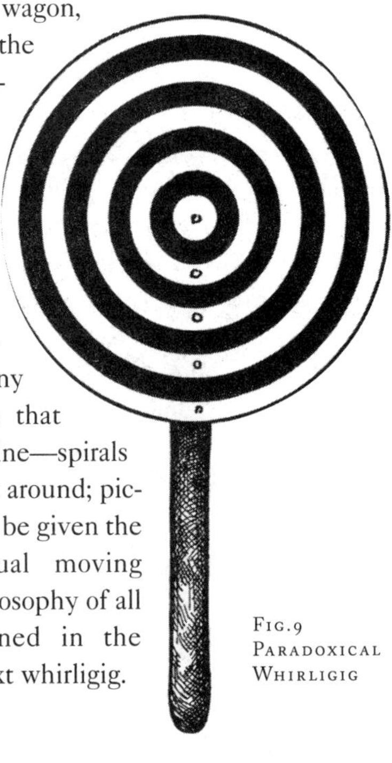

FIG. 9
PARADOXICAL
WHIRLIGIG

The Phantasmoscope, or Magic Wheel.

The phantasmoscope, or magic wheel, is comparatively simple, consisting, as may be seen by the accompanying illustration, of a disk of any diameter revolving upon a pin in the center. Figures in different poses of arrested action are painted or pasted upon the one side; under each figure is an oblong opening or slot. Much amusement can be derived from this old and simple toy. We herewith give one with the correct positions of a horse trotting a 2:40 gain, drawn in silhouette upon the outer margin of the wheel.

Make a careful tracing of the illustration (Fig. 10) with a lead-pencil upon tracing-paper; reverse the tracing-paper upon a piece of card-board so that the side with the pencil-markings on it will be next to the card-board; after which fasten both card-board and paper to a drawing-board or table-top with tacks, so that neither tracing nor card-board can slip. With the point of a hard pencil, a slate-pencil or any similar instrument, go carefully over each line of the tracing as seen through the tracing-paper; be careful not to omit a single mark; it is very provoking to discover, after removing the tracing-paper, that part of the drawing is wanting; but if you have been careful, when the tacks are removed you will find the picture neatly transferred on the card-board. Go carefully over each line on the card-board with a pen and black ink, and fill in the outlines of each picture with ink, making a silhouette of the figures.

Cut the phantasmoscope, or magic disk, out, following the outer circle with the scissors, and under each figure, where the oblong places are drawn, cut a corresponding opening through the pasteboard. Fasten the

FIG. 10 THE MAGIC WHEEL

wheel to a stick or handle by means of a pin at its cen-ter, on which it can freely turn.

If a larger machine be wanted, the illustration here given may be enlarged. To use the magic wheel, stand in front of a mirror, as shown in the small illus-tration; hold the disk before the eyes; look through the slots under the figures, and turn the wheel rapidly. The horses' legs will commence to move as in life, and as each successive position drawn upon the phantas-moscope is the exact one taken by a trotting horse, the horses in the mirror will all appear to be in actual motion, on a fast trot. If the eye is directed over the margin of the paste-board disk, an indistinct blur is all that is seen. The principle is generally well known and easily explained. It pertains to the phenomenon known as the persistence of vision. When the eye is directed through the slot, the figure of a horse is seen for an instant as the opening passes the eye, and the impression is retained after the object is shut off by the intervening portion of the board between the slots until another horse appears through the succeeding opening, when an additional impression is made, the same as the preceding impression, except a slight change in the position of the legs. These impressions follow each other so rapidly that they produce upon the retina of the eye the effect of a continuous image of the horses, in which the limbs, replaced by a succession of positions, present the appearance of a file of horses in actual motion.

The instantaneous photographs taken nowadays of people, horses, and other animals in motion, opens a new field for investigation, and one which, with the aid of the simple toy described, will be found very entertaining as well as instructive.

MAKING THE
HORSES TROT

Mr. Muybridge's celebrated photographs of animals in motion can all be adapted by smart boys to home-made phantasmoscopes, and it will probably not be long before the wonderful photographs of birds and bats on the wing, taken by E. J. Marcy with his revolving pho-tographic gun, will be within reach of the public. Then with the magic disk the reader can make birds fly, horses trot, men ride bicycles, and reproduce every movement as correct as in nature.

For young scientists these beautiful experiments will be found very entertaining.

HOW TO MAKE GIFTS OUT OF A HEAP OF RUBBISH

*I*N almost every house there is an attic, and in almost every attic may be found a room where trunks are stored, where broken toys and disabled furniture are put out of sight, and where all articles not worth selling or giving away gradually accumulate until this attic room contains, literally, a heap or rubbish. Entering one of these lumber-rooms not long ago, and glancing over the medley which comprised so much, from a tin can to a piece of broken bric-à-brac, the thought occurred to me that something might be done with it, some use be made of at least a few of the articles consigned to the place as utterly useless.

That was rather a thrifty thought. Do you not think so? Then let us make the most of it and together venture back into that mysterious and somewhat dusty chamber, and see if there really is anything there worth the making over.

In imagination we will stand in our attic lumber-room and begin to look about us with eyes and mind open to perceive possibilities.

On one side of the room, leaning against the wall, we see what was once a handsome old-fashioned mirror, quite large and of heavy plate-glass. Its poor dusty face, reflecting dimly its barren surroundings, is shattered in many pieces, and at first sight it seems hopeless to attempt to restore it to the plane of beauty or usefulness; but do not let us be hasty; we will examine it more closely. Yes, here is a piece of glass large enough to frame. Never mind its uneven shape and rough edges; we will work out that problem later. Now we must put it carefully aside and continue our investigations.

Here is a large tin can, which can be made into a lantern to hang in the hall, and this baking-powder can may be of some use, so we will take it also.

The tops of three cheese-boxes; something should be done with them. Perhaps they can be used for a table; put them with the other chosen things.

A croquet-ball! That will make a fine key-rack. This box of silks and ribbons we may need, and the large pasteboard-box will do for the foundation of our mirror frame.

We must have this piece of old brass chain this handful of large nails, the pasteboard roll which has been used for sending engravings through the mail, and that old broad-brimmed straw hat; also these three broomsticks and the piece of nice dark-gray hardware paper.

Now, seated in our own room, let us see what we can do with this rather unpromising array of objects spread around us. First we will try

THE MIRROR,

and must cast about us for the ways and means of framing it. The large pasteboard-box we have already decided will make a good foundation. After tearing off the sides, we will cut an even square from the bottom, which is smooth and unwarped.

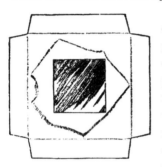

FIG. 1 BROWN PAPER PASTED
ON MIRROR AND
PASTEBOARD FOR HOME-MADE
MIRROR-FRAME

Next laying the piece of mirror on the square of pasteboard we must cut, out of ordinary brown wrapping-paper, a square two inches larger all around than the pasteboard, make a hole in the center as large as the shape of the mirror will allow, and paste it down on the mirror and pasteboard (Fig. 1). Then, after clipping out the corners, we will turn the edges over on to the back of the pasteboard foundation and paste them down. Cutting four strips of the hardware paper, about two inches wide, we will fold them through the center lengthwise and paste them around the glass, lapping them just a little over the edge of the other paper, the folded side being next to the glass (Fig. 2). This will form a bevel for our frame. From the same paper we will now cut a square, three inches larger on all sides than the foundation; then, exactly in the center, mark a square half an inch larger all around than the square of mirror showing. In the center of the square marked out we must insert our scissors, cut it like Fig. 3, and after clipping off the points, as indicated by the dotted lines L, M, O, N, turn back the four pieces at the dotted lines, P, Q, R, S,

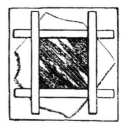

FIG. 2 BROWN BEVEL OF HARDWARE PAPER ON FRAME

leaving an open square. Then placing it over the mirror so that the same width of beveled edge shows on all sides of the mirror, we must paste it down. Clipping out the corners, as shown in diagram, we will bring the edges

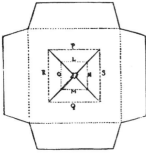

FIG. 3 THE OUTSIDE COVERING FOR MIRROR-FRAM

over and paste them down securely to the back of the frame. A piece of hardware paper, cut in a square one inch smaller than the frame, we will paste on the back to finish it off and hide the edges of the paper where they have been turned over (Fig. 4).

We must fasten on a piece of tape by which to hang the mirror, by pasting down the ends of the tape on the frame (letter T, Fig. 4), and pasting over each a strip of the hardware paper (letter U, Fig. 4). When the frame is quite dry we will paint a branch of dogwood or some light-colored flower across it, and have as pretty a little mirror as anyone could wish for.

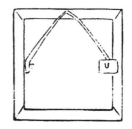

FIG. 4 BACK OF FRAME WITH TAPE ATTACHED

HOME-MADE MIRROR-FRAME

The next thing to commence will be

THE TABLE,

Which you can make yourselves by following these directions:

The three cheese-box lids will answer nicely as shelves for a work- or bric-à-brac table, and the broomsticks, which are all the same length, will do for the legs.

Upon each broomstick mark the distances for placing the shelves, allowing six inches from each end of the stick for the top and bottom, and the exact center between these points for the middle shelf. With a pocket-knife cut narrow grooves around each stick, one-half inch on either side of the points marked on them (Fig. 5). This will make six grooves on each stick. Now measure the box-lids to find their circumferences, and divide them into thirds, marking the distances on the rim to obtain the true position for the legs. At these points bore four holes with a gimlet, one inch apart, two above and two below (Fig. 6). Through one of the top holes pass a piece of pliable wire, place one of the broomsticks against the

FIG. 5 NARROW GROOVES CUT AROUND BROOMSTICK FOR TABLE-LEG

FIG. 6 HOLES BORED IN A BOX-LID USED AS A TABLE-SHELF

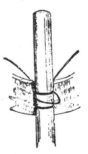

FIG. 7 MANNER OF FASTENING A SHELF TO TABLE-LEG

rim of the lid, pass the wire back through the other upper hole (Fig. 7), fit it into the upper groove of the stick, and draw it tight.

Fig. 8 Table-shelf and
Leg Fastened securely
together by Wire

Twice the wire must be put through the upper holes and around the stick in the top groove; then, bringing it down on the inside of the lid, you must put it twice through the lower holes and around the stick in the lower groove; then twist the ends and tuck them under the wire on the inside of the lid (Fig 8). In this way each leg will have to be fastened to each shelf. When the table is all put together paint it black, and, as soon as it is dry, tie a bright ribbon on one of the sticks at the top, and a charming little bric-à-brac table will be the result of your labor.

You can make a very pretty

Lantern

of the old tin can; but first you must have some tools to work with; not many, only a piece of wood, rounded on one side to fit into the can, a hatchet or heavy hammer, and a few wrought iron nails. If the piece of wood is not large enough to fit the can, another stick can be put in to hold the first one firmly against the can. That being arranged, you must decide upon some kind of pattern to made by the holds, and indicate it on the can with a small paint-brush and paint or ink; then, laying the can on its side, the rounded piece of wood being at the top, with one of the wrought iron nails puncture the holes where you have indicated the pattern. With the hammer drive the nail through the tin into the wood; then draw it out, make another hole, and so on until all holes you wish are driven through that part of the can held in place by the rounded piece of wood.

This wood, you see, keeps the can from bending when the nail is being driven through. In moving the wood as the work progresses, you must always keep it under that part of the can being punctured. To make the large hold, you will have to put a number of the small holes close together, and then drive the nail through the partitions, cutting them away. The pattern being completed, puncture three holes, close to the top of the can, at equal distances apart. These are for the chains to pass through, by which to suspend the lantern. In the cover of the baking-powder can make three holes at equal distances; then divide the chain, which is about one yard and a quarter long, into three equal lengths, separating the pieces by prying open the links. Put an end of each piece through the holes made for them at the top of the can, and fasten them by hooking the open links through the links of the chain a little farther up, and hammering them together again.

LANTERN

Now pass the ends of the chains through the holes made in the lid of the baking-powder can, and, bringing the ends together, fasten them by joining the links.

Paint the lantern, chain and all, black, and while it is drying make a stand for the candle which is to furnish the light. A square piece of thin board, just large enough

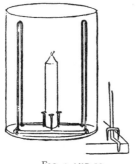

to fit into the can without touching the sides will do for the stand. Drive four small nails in the center to hold the candle (Fig. 9).

Make handles for lifting the stand in and out of the lantern, by bending two pieces of wire like Fig. 9, and fastening them to the board with staple tacks (Fig. 10).

FIG. 9 AND 10
STAND IN LANTERN, WITH
NAILS FOR HOLDING CANDLE

When the paint on the lantern is dry, paste red tissue-paper all around the inside to give a cheerful red glow to the light, which will shine through it. If you would like it to resemble a jeweled lantern, paste different colored papers over the large holes and leave the small ones open. An S hook passed through the loop made by the three chains will serve to connect them to the chain which should suspend the lantern from the ceiling.

A MUSIC-ROLL

can be made of the pasteboard roll.

Cut a round piece of pasteboard just the size to fit into one end of the roll; then cut out another round

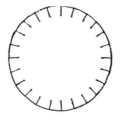

FIG. 11
PAPER COVERING FOR END
OF MUSIC-ROLL

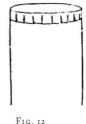

FIG. 12
PAPER PASTED OVER END
OF MUSIC-ROLL

piece, this time of paper, one inch larger than that made of pasteboard. Clip the edges (Fig. 11) and paste it over the end of the roll which is filled in with the round of pasteboard (Fig. 12).

Among the scraps of silk and ribbons you will, perhaps, find a good-sized piece of dark-green or brown silk; use this for the case, which must cover the roll neatly. To make the case fit the end of the roll you have just filled up, mark on a piece of the silk a circle the size of that end of the roll. This can be done by standing the roll on the silk, and running a pencil around the edge. When cutting out the silk leave a margin of a quarter of an inch on the outside of the pencil-mark for the seam. Cur the silk for covering the roll three inches longer than the roll, and wide enough to allow for a quarter of an inch seam. Sew up the long seam, and then sew the round of silk into the end of the case. Hem the other end of the case, and run in a narrow ribbon about an inch from the edge. This is for a draw-string.

When the roll is fitted snugly in its case, tie a ribbon, matching it in color, around the roll, making a loop to form the handle. Fasten the ribbon by taking a few stitches under the bows, catching them on to the silk.

MUSIC-ROLL

The old straw hat can be transformed into a dainty

Work-Basket

It is stiff and harsh at present, but pour boiling water over it and the straw will become soft and pliable, and can be bent into any shape you like. When dry, it will be again stiff, and will retain the form you have given it. After scalding the hat bend the brim in toward the center, in four different places, at equal distances apart. This will make a fluted basket. You must tie it in shape (Fig. 13) and leave until perfectly dry; then bronze the basket, line it with Silesia, and sew silk or satin around the top to form a bag. Run a draw-string of

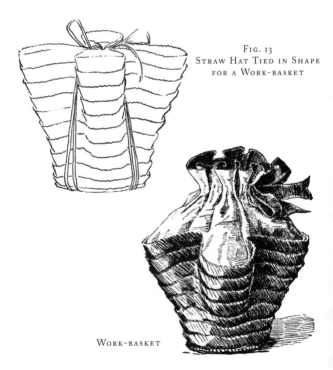

Fig. 13
Straw Hat Tied in Shape
for a Work-basket

Work-basket

narrow ribbon near the top of the bag, and the pretty little work-basket is finished.

The croquet ball you can make into a

KEY AND BUTTON-HOOK RACK

First you must gild it, and then around the middle of the ball, at regular intervals, insert small brass hooks. A yellow ribbon and bow, tacked on the top with small tacks, will serve to suspend it by, and completes the rack.

KEY RACK

With the gild left from gilding the ball, and a piece of bright ribbon you can make a

PAPER-WEIGHT

of six of the large nails. Gild each nail separately, let them dry, and then tie them securely together with a piece of ribbon.

PAPER-WEIGHT

All the articles brought from the attic have now been turned to some use, but there are many other things to be found there which we have not space to mention, and which with little trouble can be so transformed that no one would ever suppose they were originally from a heap of rubbish.

THE CHRISTMAS FAIRY
by John Strange Winter

*I*T was getting very near to Christmas-time, and all the boys at Miss Ware's school were talking excitedly about going home for the holidays, of the fun they would have, the presents they would receive on Christmas morning, the tips from Grannies, Uncles, and Aunts, of the pantomimes, the parties, the never-ending joys and pleasures which would be theirs.

"I shall go to Madame Tussaud's and to the Drury Lane pantomime," said the young Fellowes, "and my mother will give a party, and Aunt Adelaide will give another, and Johnny Sanderson and Mary Greville, and ever so many others. I shall have a splendid time at home. Oh! Jim, I wish it were all holidays like it is when one's grown up."

"My Uncle Bob is going to give me a pair of skates—clippers," remarked Harry Wadham.

"My father's going to give me a bike," put in George Alderson.

"Will you bring it back to school with you?" asked Harry.

"Oh! Yes, I should think so, if Miss Ware doesn't say no."

"I say, Shivers," cried Fellowes, "where are you going to spend your holidays?"

"I'm going to stop here," answered the boy called Shivers, in a very forlorn tome.

"Here—with old Ware?—oh, my! Why can't you go home?"

"I can't go home to India," answered Shivers—his real name, by the bye, was Egerton, Tom Egerton.

"No—who said you could? But haven't you any relations anywhere?"

Shivers shook his head. "Only in India," he said miserably.

"Poor old chap; that's rough luck for you. Oh, I'll tell you what it is, you fellows, if I couldn't go home for the holidays—especially at Christmas—I think I'd just sit down and die."

"Oh! No, you wouldn't," said Shivers; "you'd hate it, and you'd get ever so home-sick and miserable, but you wouldn't die over it. You'd just get through some-how, and hope something would happen before next year, or that some kind fairy or other would—"

"Bosh! There are no fairies nowadays," said Fellowes. "See here, Shivers, I'll write home and ask my mother if she won't invite you to come back with me for the holidays."

"Will you really?"

"Yes, I will: and if she says yes, we shall have such a splendid time, because, you know, we live in London, and go to everything, and have heaps of tips and parties and fun."

"Perhaps she will say no," suggested poor little Shivers, who had steeled himself to the idea that there would be no Christmas holidays for him, excepting that he would have no lessons for so many weeks.

"My mother isn't at all the kind of woman who says no," Fellowes declared loudly.

In a few days' time, however, a letter arrived from his mother, which he opened eagerly.

"My own darling boy," it said, "I am so very sorry to have to tell you that dear little Aggie is down with scarlet fever, and so you cannot come home for your holidays, not yet bring your young friend with you, as I would have loved you to do if all had been well here. Your Aunt Adelaide would have had you there, but her two girls have both got scarlatine—and I believe Aggie got hers there, though, of course, poor Aunt Adelaide could not help it. I did think about your going to Cousin Rachel's. She most kindly offered to invite you, but, dear boy, she is an old lady, and so particular, and not used to boys, and she lives so far from anything which is going on that you would be able to go to nothing, so your father and I came to the conclusion that the very best thing that you could do under the circumstances is for you to stay at Miss Ware's and for us to send your Christmas to you as well as we can. It won't be like being at home, darling boy, but you will try and be happy—won't you, and make me feel that you are helping me in this dreadful time. Dear little Aggie is very ill, very ill indeed. We have two nurses. Nora and Connie are shut away in the morning-room and to the back stairs and their own rooms with Miss Ellis, and have not seen us since the dear child was first taken ill. Tell your young friend that I am sending you a hamper from Buszard's, with double of everything, and I am writing to Miss Ware to ask her to take you both to anything that may be going on in Cross Hampton. And tell him that it makes me so much happier to think that you won't be alone.—

"Your own Mother."

"This letter will smell queer, darling; it will be fumigated before posting."

It must be owned that when Bertie Fellowes received this letter, which was neither more nor less than a shattering of all his Christmas hopes and joys, that he fairly broke down, and hiding his face upon his arms as they rested on his desk, sobbed aloud. The forlorn boy from India, who sat next to him, tried every boyish means of consolation that he could think of. He patted his shoulder, whispered many pitying words, and, at last, flung his arm across him and hugged him tightly, as, poor little chap, he himself many times since his arrival in England, had *wished* someone would do to him.

At last Bertie Fellowes thrust his mother's letter into his friend's hand. "Read it," he sobbed.

So Shivers made himself a master of Mrs. Fellowes' letter and understood the cause of the boy's outburst of grief. "Old fellow," he said at last, "don't fret over it. It might be worse. Why, you might be like me, with your father and mother thousands of miles away. When Aggie is better, you'll be able to go home—and it'll help your mother if she things you are *almost* as happy as if you were at home. It must be worse for her—she has cried ever so over her letter—see, it's all tear-blots."

The troubles and disappointments of youth are bitter while they last, but they soon pass, and the sun shines again. By the time Miss Ware, who was a kind-hearted, sensible, pleasant woman, came to tell Fellowes how sorry she was for him and his disappointment, the worst had gone by, and the boy was resigned to what could not be helped.

"Well, after all, one man's meat is another man's poison," she said, smiling down on the two boys; "poor Tom has been looking forward to spending his holidays all alone with us, and now he will have a friend with him. Try to look on the bright side, Bertie, and to remember how much worse it would have been if there had been no boy to stay with you."

"I can't help being disappointed, Miss Ware," said Bertie, his eyes filling afresh and his lips quivering.

"No, dear boy, you would be anything but a nice boy if you were not. But I want you to try and think of your poor mother, who is full of trouble and anxiety, and to write to her as brightly as you can, and tell her not to worry about you more than she can help."

"Yes," said Bertie; but he turned his head away, and it was evident to the school-mistress that his heart was too full to let him say more.

Still, he was a good boy, Bertie Fellowes, and when he wrote home to his mother it was quite a bright every-day kind of letter, telling her how sorry he was about Aggie, and detailing a few of the ways in which he and Shivers meant to spend their holidays. His letter ended thus:—

"Shivers got a letter from his mother yesterday with three pounds in it: if you happen to see Uncle Dick, will you tell him I want a 'Waterbury' dreadfully?"

The last day of the term came, and one by one, or two by two, the various boys went away, until at last only Bertie Fellowes and Shivers were left in the great house. It had never appeared so large to either of them before. The schoolroom seemed to have grown to about the size of a church, the dining-room, set now with only one table instead of three was not like the same, while the dormitory, which had never before had any room to spare, was like a wilderness. To Bertie Fellowes it was all dreary and wretched—to the boy from India, who knew no other house in England, no other thought came than that it was a blessing that he had one companion left. "It is miserable," groaned poor Bertie as they strolled into the great echoing school-room after a lonely tea, set at one corner of the smallest of the three dining-tables; "just think if we had been on our way home now—how different!"

"Just think if I had been left here by myself," said Shivers—and he gave a shiver which fully justified his name.

"Yes—but—" began Bertie, then shamefacedly and with a blush, added, "you know, when one wants to go home ever so badly, one never thinks that some chaps haven't got a home to go to."

The evening went by—discipline was relapsed entirely and the two boys went to bed in the top empty dormitory, and told stories to each other for a long time before they went to sleep. That night Bertie Fellowes dreamt of Madame Tussaud's and the great pantomime at Drury Lane, and poor Shivers of a long creeper-covered bungalow far away in the shining East, and they both cried a little under the bed-clothes. Yet each put a brave face on their desolate circumstances to the other, and so another day began.

This was the day before Christmas Eve, that delightful day of preparation for the greatest festival in all the year—the day when in most households there are many little mysteries afoot, when parcels come and go, and are smothered away so as to be ready when Santa Clause comes his rounds; when some are busy decking the rooms with holly and mistletoe; when the cook is busiest of all, and savory smells rise from the kitchen, telling of good things to be eaten on the morrow.

There were some preparations on foot at Minchin House, though there was not the same bustle and noise as is to be found in a large family. And quite early in the morning came the great hamper of which Mrs. Fellowes had spoken in her letter to Bertie. Then just as the early dinner had come to an end, and Miss Ware was telling the two boys that she would take them round the town to look at the shops, there was a tremendous peal at the bell of the front door, and a voice was heard asking for Master Egerton. In a trice Shivers had sprung to his feet, his face quite white, his hands trembling, and the next moment the door was thrown open, and a tall handsome lady came in, to whom he flew with a sobbing cry of "Aunt Laura! Aunt Laura!"

Aunt Laura explained in less time that it takes me to write this, that her husband, Colonel Desmond, had had left to him a large fortune and that they had come as soon as possible to England, having, in fact, only arrived in London the previous day. "I was so afraid, Tom darling," she said in ending, "that we should not get here till Christmas Day was over, and I was so afraid you might be disappointed, that I would not let Mother tell you we were on our way home. I have brought a letter from Mother to Miss Ware—and you must get your things packed up at once and come back with me by the six o'clock train to town. Then Uncle Jack and I will take you everywhere, and give you a splendid time, you dear little chap, here all by yourself."

For a minute or two Shivers' face was radiant; then he caught sight of Bertie's down-drooped mouth, and turned to his Aunt.

"Dear Aunt Laura," he said, holding her hand very fast with his own, "I'm awfully sorry, but I can't go."

"Can't go? And why not?"

"Because I can't go and leave Fellowes here all alone," he said stoutly, though he could scarcely keep a suspicious quaver out of his voice. "When I was going to be alone, Fellowes wrote and asked his mother to let me go home with him, and she couldn't, because his sister has got scarlet fever, and they daren't have either of us; and he's got to stay here—and he's never been away at Christmas before—and—and—I can't go away and leave him by himself, Aunt Laura—and—"

For the space of a moment or so, Mrs. Desmond stared at the boy as if she could not believe her ears; then she caught hold of him and half smothered him with kisses.

"Bless you, you dear little chap, you shall not leave him: you shall bring him along and we'll all enjoy ourselves together. What's his name?—Bertie Fellowes! Bertie, my man, you are not very old yet, so I'm going to teach you a lesson as well as ever I can—it is that kindness is never wasted in this world. I'll go out now and telegraph to your mother—I don't suppose she will refuse to let you come with us."

A couple of hours later she returned in triumph, waving a telegram to the two excited boys.

"God bless you, yes, with all our hearts," it ran; *"you have taken a load off our minds."*

And so Bertie Fellowes and Shivers found that there was such a thing as a fairy after all.

A CHRISTMAS DREAM,
AND HOW IT CAME TRUE

I'M SO tired of Christmas I wish there never would be another one!" exclaimed a discontented-looking little girl, as she sat idly watching her mother arrange a pile of gifts two days before they were to be given.

"Why, Effie, what a dreadful thing to say! You are as bad as old Scrooge; and I'm afraid something will happen to you, as it did to him, if you don't care for dear Christmas," answered mamma, almost dropping the silver horn she was filling with delicious candies.

"Who was Scrooge? What happened to him?" asked Effie, with a glimmer of interest in her listless face, as she picked out the sourest lemon-drop she could find; for nothing sweet suited her just then.

"He was one of Dickens's best people, and you can read the charming story some day. He hated Christmas until a strange dream showed him how dear and beautiful it was, and made a better man of him."

"I shall read it; for I like dreams, and have a great many curious ones myself. But they don't keep me from being tired of Christmas," said Effie, poking discontentedly among the sweeties for something worth eating.

"Why are you tired of what should be the happiest time of all the year?" asked mamma, anxiously.

"Perhaps I shouldn't be if I had something new. But it is always the same, and there isn't any more surprise about it. I always find heaps of goodies in my stocking. Don't like some of them, and soon get tired of those I do like. We always have a great dinner, and I eat too much, and feel ill next day. Then there is a Christmas tree somewhere, with a doll on top, or a stupid old Santa Claus, and children dancing and screaming over bonbons and toys that break, and shiny things that are of no use. Really, mamma, I've had so many Christmases all alike that I don't think I can bear another one." And Effie laid herself flat on the sofa, as if the mere idea was too much for her.

Her mother laughed at her despair, but was sorry to see her little girl so discontented, when she had everything to make her happy, and had known but ten Christmas days.

"Suppose we don't give you any presents at all,—how would that suit you?" asked mamma, anxious to please her spoiled child.

"I should like one large and splendid one, and one dear little one, to remember some very nice person by," said Effie, who was a fanciful little body, full of odd whims and notions, which her friends loved to gratify, regardless of time, trouble, or money; for she was the last of three little girls, and very dear to all the family.

"Well, my darling, I will see what I can do to please you, and not say a word until all is ready. If I could only get a new idea to start with!" And mamma went on tying up her pretty bundles with a thoughtful face, while Effie strolled to the window to watch the rain that kept her in-doors and made her dismal.

"Seems to me poor children have better times than rich ones. I can't go out, and there is a girl about my age splashing along, without any maid to fuss about rubbers and cloaks and umbrellas and colds. I wish I was a beggar-girl."

"Would you like to be hungry, cold, and ragged, to beg all day, and sleep on an ash-heap at night?" asked mamma, wondering what would come next.

"Cinderella did, and had a nice time in the end. This girl out here has a basket of scraps on her arm, and a big old shawl all round her, and doesn't seem to care a bit, though the water runs out of the toes of her boots. She goes paddling along, laughing at the rain, and eating a cold potato as if it tasted nicer than the chicken and ice-cream I had for dinner. Yes, I do think poor children are happier than rich ones."

"So do I, sometimes. At the Orphan Asylum today I saw two dozen merry little souls who have no parents, no home, and no hope of Christmas beyond a stick of candy or a cake. I wish you had been there to see how happy they were, playing with the old toys some richer children had sent them."

"You may give them all mine; I'm so tired of them I never want to see them again," said Effie, turning from the window to the pretty baby-house full of everything a child's heart could desire.

"I will, and let you begin again with something you will not tire of, if I can only find it." And mamma knit her brows trying to discover some grand surprise for this child who didn't care for Christmas.

Nothing more was said then; and wandering off to the library, Effie found "A Christmas Carol," and curling herself up in the sofa corner, read it all before tea. Some of it she did not understand; but she laughed and cried over many parts of the charming story, and felt better without knowing why.

All the evening she thought of poor Tiny Tim, Mrs. Cratchit with the pudding, and the stout old gentleman who danced so gayly that "his legs twinkled in the air." Presently bedtime arrived.

"Come, now, and toast your feet," said Effie's nurse, "while I do your pretty hair and tell stories."

"I'll have a fairy tale to-night, a very interesting one," commanded Effie, as she put on her blue silk wrapper and little fur-lined slippers to sit before the fire and have her long curls brushed.

So Nursey told her best tales; and when at last the child lay down under her lace curtains, her head was full of a curious jumble of Christmas elves, poor children, snow-storms, sugarplums, and surprises. So it is no wonder that she dreamed all night; and this was the dream, which she never quite forgot.

She found herself sitting on a stone, in the middle of a great field, all alone. The snow was falling fast, a bitter wind whistled by, and night was coming on. She felt hungry, cold, and tired, and did not know where to go nor what to do.

"I wanted to be a beggar-girl, and now I am one; but I don't like it, and wish somebody would come and take care of me. I don't know who I am, and I think I must be lost," thought Effie, with the curious interest one takes in one's self in dreams.

But the more she thought about it, the more bewildered she felt. Faster fell the snow, colder blew the wind, darker grew the night; and poor Effie made up her mind that she was quite forgotten and left to freeze alone.

The tears were chilled on her cheeks, her feet felt like icicles, and her heart died within her, so hungry, frightened, and forlorn was she. Laying her head on her knees, she gave herself up for lost, and sat there with the great flakes fast turning her to a little white mound, when suddenly the sound of music reached her, and starting up, she looked and listened with all her eyes and ears.

Far away a dim light shone, and a voice was heard singing. She tried to run toward the welcome glimmer, but could not stir, and stood like a small statue of expectation while the light drew nearer, and the sweet words of the song grew clearer.

From our happy home
Through the world we roam
One week in all the year,
    Making winter spring
    With the joy we bring,
For Christmas-tide is here.

    Now the eastern star
    Shines from afar
To light the poorest home;
    Hearts warmer grow,
    Gifts freely flow,
For Christmas-tide has come.

    Now gay trees rise
    Before young eyes,
Abloom with tempting cheer;
    Blithe voices sing,
    And blithe bells ring,
For Christmas-tide is here.

    Oh, happy chime,
    Oh, blessed time,
That draws us all so near!
    "Welcome, dear day,"
    All creatures say,
For Christmas-tide is here.

A child's voice sang, a child's hand carried the little candle; and in the circle of soft light it shed, Effie saw a pretty child coming to her through the night and snow. A rosy, smiling creature, wrapped in white fur, with a wreath of green and scarlet holly on its shining hair, the magic candle in one hand, and the other outstretched as if to shower gifts and warmly press all other hands.

Effie forgot to speak as this bright vision came nearer, leaving no trace of footsteps in the snow, only lighting the way with its little candle, and filling the air with the music of its song.

"Dear child, you are lost, and I have come to find you," said the stranger, taking Effie's cold hands in his, with a smile like sunshine, while every holly berry glowed like a little fire.

"Do you know me?" asked Effie, feeling no fear, but a great gladness, at his coming.

"I know all children, and go to find them; for this is my holiday, and I gather them from all parts of the world to be merry with me once a year."

"Are you an angel?" asked Effie, looking for the wings.

"No; I am a Christmas spirit, and live with my mates in a pleasant place, getting ready for our holiday, when we are let out to roam about the world, helping make this a happy time for all who will let us in. Will you come and see how we work?"

"I will go anywhere with you. Don't leave me again," cried Effie, gladly.

"First I will make you comfortable. That is what we love to do. You are cold, and you shall be warm, hungry, and I will feed you; sorrowful, and I will make you gay."

With a wave of his candle all three miracles were wrought,—for the snow- flakes turned to a white fur cloak and hood on Effie's head and shoulders, a bowl of hot soup came sailing to her lips, and vanished when she had eagerly drunk the last drop; and suddenly the dismal field changed to a new world so full of wonders that all her troubles were forgotten in a minute.

Bells were ringing so merrily that it was hard to keep from dancing. Green garlands hung on the walls, and every tree was a Christmas tree full of toys, and blazing with candles that never went out.

In one place many little spirits sewed like mad on warm clothes, turning off work faster than any sewing-machine ever invented, and great piles were made ready to be sent to poor people. Other busy creatures packed money into purses, and wrote checks which they sent flying away on the wind,—a lovely kind of snow-storm to fall into a world below full of poverty.

Older and graver spirits were looking over piles of little books, in which the records of the past year were kept, telling how different people had spent it, and what sort of gifts they deserved. Some got peace, some disappointment, some remorse and sorrow, some great joy and hope. The rich had generous thoughts sent them; the poor, gratitude and contentment. Children had more love and duty to parents; and parents renewed patience, wisdom, and satisfaction for and in their children. No one was forgotten.

"Please tell me what splendid place this is?" asked Effie, as soon as she could collect her wits after the first look at all these astonishing things.

"This is the Christmas world; and here we work all the year round, never tired of getting ready for the happy day. See, these are the saints just setting off; for some have far to go, and the children must not be disappointed."

As he spoke the spirit pointed to four gates, out of which four great sleighs were just driving, laden with toys, while a jolly old Santa Claus sat in the middle of each, drawing on his mittens and tucking up his wraps for a long cold drive.

"Why, I thought there was only one Santa Claus, and even he was a humbug," cried Effie, astonished at the sight.

"Never give up your faith in the sweet old stones, even after you come to see that they are only the pleasant shadow of a lovely truth."

Just then the sleighs went off with a great jingling of bells and pattering of reindeer hoofs, while all the spirits gave a cheer that was heard in the lower world, where people said, "Hear the stars sing."

"I never will say there isn't any Santa Claus again. Now, show me more."

"You will like to see this place, I think, and may learn something here perhaps"

The spirit smiled as he led the way to a little door, through which Effie peeped into a world of dolls. Baby-houses were in full blast, with dolls of all sorts going on like live people. Waxen ladies sat in their parlors elegantly dressed; black dolls cooked in the kitchens; nurses walked out with the bits of dollies; and the streets were full of tin soldiers marching, wooden horses prancing, express wagons rumbling, and little men hurrying to and fro. Shops were there, and tiny people buying legs of mutton, pounds of tea, mites of clothes, and everything dolls use or wear or want.

But presently she saw that in some ways the dolls improved upon the manners and customs of human beings, and she watched eagerly to learn why they did these things. A fine Paris doll driving in her carriage took up a black worsted Dinah who was hobbling along with a basket of clean clothes, and carried her to her journey's end, as if it were the proper thing to do.

Another interesting china lady took off her comfortable red cloak and put it round a poor wooden creature done up in a paper shift, and so badly painted that its face would have sent some babies into fits.

"Seems to me I once knew a rich girl who didn't give her things to poor girls. I wish I could remember who she was, and tell her to be as kind as that china doll," said Effie, much touched at the sweet way the pretty creature wrapped up the poor fright, and then ran off in her little gray gown to buy a shiny fowl stuck on a wooden platter for her invalid mother's dinner.

"We recall these things to people's minds by dreams. I think the girl you speak of won't forget this one." And the spirit smiled, as if he enjoyed some joke which she did not see.

A little bell rang as she looked, and away scampered the children into the red-and-green schoolhouse with the roof that lifted up, so one could see how nicely they sat at their desks with mites of books, or drew on the inch-square blackboards with crumbs of chalk.

"They know their lessons very well, and are as still as mice. We make a great racket at our school, and get bad marks every day. I shall tell the girls they had better mind what they do, or their dolls will be better scholars than they are," said Effie, much impressed, as she peeped in and saw no rod in the hand of the little mistress, who looked up and shook her head at the intruder, as if begging her to go away before the order of the school was disturbed.

Effie retired at once, but could not resist one look in at the window of a fine mansion, where the family were at dinner, the children behaved so well at table, and never grumbled a bit when their mamma said they could not have any more fruit.

"Now, show me something else," she said, as they came again to the low door that led out of Doll-land.

"You have seen how we prepare for Christmas; let me show you where we love best to send our good and happy gifts," answered the spirit, giving her his hand again.

"I know. I've seen ever so many," began Effie, thinking of her own Christmases.

"No, you have never seen what I will show you. Come away, and remember what you see to-night."

Like a flash that bright world vanished, and Effie found herself in a part of the city she had never seen before. It was far away from the gayer places, where every store was brilliant with lights and full of pretty things, and every house wore a festival air, while people hurried to and fro with merry greetings. It was down among the dingy streets where the poor lived, and where there was no making ready for Christmas.

Hungry women looked in at the shabby shops, longing to buy meat and bread, but empty pockets forbade. Tipsy men drank up their wages in the bar-rooms; and in many cold dark chambers little children huddled under the thin blankets, trying to forget their misery in sleep.

No nice dinners filled the air with savory smells, no gay trees dropped toys and bonbons into eager hands, no little stockings hung in rows beside the chimney-piece ready to be filled, no happy sounds of music, gay voices, and dancing feet were heard; and there were no signs of Christmas anywhere.

"Don't they have any in this place?" asked Effie, shivering, as she held fast the spirit's hand, following where he led her.

"We come to bring it. Let me show you our best workers." And the spirit pointed to some sweet-faced men and women who came stealing into the poor houses, working such beautiful miracles that Effie could only stand and watch.

Some slipped money into the empty pockets, and sent the happy mothers to buy all the comforts they needed; others led the drunken men out of temptation, and took them home to find safer pleasures there. Fires were kindled on cold hearths, tables spread as if by magic, and warm clothes wrapped round shivering limbs. Flowers suddenly bloomed in the chambers of the sick; old people found themselves remembered; sad hearts were consoled by a tender word, and wicked ones softened by the story of Him who forgave all sin.

But the sweetest work was for the children; and Effie held her breath to watch these human fairies hang up and fill the little stockings without which a child's Christmas is not perfect, putting in things that once she would have thought very humble presents, but which now seemed beautiful and precious because these poor babies had nothing.

"That is so beautiful! I wish I could make merry Christmases as these good people do, and be loved and thanked as they are," said Effie, softly, as she watched the busy men and women do their work and steal away without thinking of any reward but their own satisfaction.

"You can if you will. I have shown you the way. Try it, and see how happy your own holiday will be hereafter."

As he spoke, the spirit seemed to put his arms about her, and vanished with a kiss.

"Oh, stay and show me more!" cried Effie, trying to hold him fast.

"Darling, wake up, and tell me why you are smiling in your sleep," said a voice in her ear; and opening her eyes, there was mamma bending over her, and morning sunshine streaming into the room.

"Are they all gone? Did you hear the bells? Wasn't it splendid?" she asked, rubbing her eyes, and looking about her for the pretty child who was so real and sweet.

"You have been dreaming at a great rate,—talking in your sleep, laughing, and clapping your hands as if you were cheering some one. Tell me what was so splendid," said mamma, smoothing the tumbled hair and lifting up the sleepy head.

Then, while she was being dressed, Effie told her dream, and Nursey thought it very wonderful; but mamma smiled to see how curiously things the child had thought, read, heard, and seen through the day were mixed up in her sleep.

"The spirit said I could work lovely miracles if I tried; but I don't know how to begin, for I have no magic candle to make feasts appear, and light up groves of Christmas trees, as he did," said Effie, sorrowfully.

"Yes, you have. We will do it! we will do it!" And

clapping her hands, mamma suddenly began to dance all over the room as if she had lost her wits.

"How? how? You must tell me, mamma," cried Effie, dancing after her, and ready to believe anything possible when she remembered the adventures of the past night.

"I've got it! I've got it!—the new idea. A splendid one, if I can only carry it out!" And mamma waltzed the little girl round till her curls flew wildly in the air, while Nursey laughed as if she would die.

"Tell me! tell me!" shrieked Effie. "No, no; it is a surprise,—a grand surprise for Christmas day!" sung mamma, evidently charmed with her happy thought. "Now, come to breakfast; for we must work like bees if we want to play spirits tomorrow. You and Nursey will go out shopping, and get heaps of things, while I arrange matters behind the scenes."

They were running downstairs as mamma spoke, and Effie called out breathlessly,—"It won't be a surprise; for I know you are going to ask some poor children here, and have a tree or something. It won't be like my dream; for they had ever so many trees, and more children than we can find anywhere. There will be no tree, no party, no dinner, in this house at all, and no presents for you. Won't that be a surprise?" And mamma laughed at Effie's bewildered face. "Do it. I shall like it, I think; and I won't ask any questions, so it will all burst upon me when the time comes," she said; and she ate her breakfast thoughtfully, for this really would be a new sort of Christmas. All that morning Effie trotted after Nursey in and out of shops, buying dozens of barking dogs, woolly lambs, and squeaking birds; tiny tea-sets, gay picture-books, mittens and hoods, dolls and candy. Parcel after parcel was sent home; but when Effie returned she saw no trace of them, though she peeped everywhere. Nursey chuckled, but wouldn't give a hint, and went out again in the afternoon with a long list of more things to buy; while Effie wandered forlornly about the house, missing the usual merry stir that went before the Christmas dinner and the evening fun.

As for mamma, she was quite invisible all day, and came in at night so tired that she could only lie on the sofa to rest, smiling as if some very pleasant thought made her happy in spite of weariness.

"Is the surprise going on all right?" asked Effie, anxiously; for it seemed an immense time to wait till another evening came.

"Beautifully! better than I expected; for several of my good friends are helping, or I couldn't have done it as I wish. I know you will like it, dear, and long remember this new way of making Christmas merry."

Mamma gave her a very tender kiss, and Effie went to bed.

The next day was a very strange one; for when she woke there was no stocking to examine, no pile of gifts under her napkin, no one said "Merry Christmas!" to her, and the dinner was just as usual to her. Mamma vanished again, and Nursey kept wiping her eyes and saying: "The dear things! It's the prettiest idea I ever heard of. No one but your blessed ma could have done it."

"Do stop, Nursey, or I shall go crazy because I don't know the secret!" cried Effie, more than once; and she kept her eye on the clock, for at seven in the evening the surprise was to come off.

The longed-for hour arrived at last, and the child was too excited to ask questions when Nurse put on her cloak and hood, led her to the carriage, and they drove away, leaving their house the one dark and silent one in the row.

"I feel like the girls in the fairy tales who are led off

to strange places and see fine things," said Effie, in a whisper, as they jingled through the gay streets.

"Ah, my deary, it is like a fairy tale, I do assure you, and you will see finer things than most children will tonight. Steady, now, and do just as I tell you, and don't say one word whatever you see," answered Nursey, quite quivering with excitement as she patted a large box in her lap, and nodded and laughed with twinkling eyes.

They drove into a dark yard, and Effie was led through a back door to a little room, where Nurse coolly proceeded to take off not only her cloak and hood, but her dress and shoes also. Effie stared and bit her lips, but kept still until out of the box came a little white fur coat and boots, a wreath of holly leaves and berries, and a candle with a frill of gold paper round it. A long "Oh!" escaped her then; and when she was dressed and saw herself in the glass, she started back, exclaiming, "Why, Nursey, I look like the spirit in my dream!"

"So you do; and that's the part you are to play, my pretty! Now whist, while I blind your eyes and put you in your place."

"Shall I be afraid?" whispered Effie, full of wonder; for as they went out she heard the sound of many voices, the tramp of many feet, and, in spite of the bandage, was sure a great light shone upon her when she stopped.

"You needn't be; I shall stand close by, and your ma will be there."

After the handkerchief was tied about her eyes, Nurse led Effie up some steps, and placed her on a high platform, where something like leaves touched her head, and the soft snap of lamps seemed to fill the air.

Music began as soon as Nurse clapped her hands, the voices outside sounded nearer, and the tramp was evidently coming up the stairs.

"Now, my precious, look and see how you and your

dear ma have made a merry Christmas for them that
needed it!"

Off went the bandage; and for a minute Effie really did think she was asleep again, for she actually stood
in "a grove of Christmas trees," all gay and shining as in
her vision. Twelve on a side, in two rows down the
room, stood the little pines, each on its low table; and
behind Effie a taller one rose to the roof, hung with
wreaths of popcorn, apples, oranges, horns of candy, and
cakes of all sorts, from sugary hearts to gingerbread
Jumbos. On the smaller trees she saw many of her own
discarded toys and those Nursey bought, as well as
heaps that seemed to have rained down straight from
that delightful Christmas country where she felt as if
she was again.

"How splendid! Who is it for? What is that noise? Where is mamma?" cried Effie, pale with pleasure and surprise, as she stood looking down the brilliant little street from her high place.

Before Nurse could answer, the doors at the lower end flew open, and in marched twenty-four little blue-gowned orphan girls, singing sweetly, until amazement changed the song to cries of joy and wonder as the shining spectacle appeared. While they stood staring with round eyes at the wilderness of pretty things about them, mamma stepped up beside Effie, and holding her hand fast to give her courage, told the story of the dream in a few simple words, ending in this way:—

"So my little girl wanted to be a Christmas spirit too, and make this a happy day for those who had not as many pleasures and comforts as she has. She likes surprises, and we planned this for you all. She shall play the good fairy, and give each of you something from this tree, after which every one will find her own name on a small tree, and can go to enjoy it in her own way. March by, my dears, and let us fill your hands."

Nobody told them to do it, but all the hands were clapped heartily before a single child stirred; then one by one they came to look up wonderingly at the pretty giver of the feast as she leaned down to offer them great yellow oranges, red apples, bunches of grapes, bonbons, and cakes, till all were gone, and a double row of smiling faces turned toward her as the children filed back to their places in the orderly way they had been taught.

Then each was led to her own tree by the good ladies who had helped mamma with all their hearts; and the happy hubbub that arose would have satisfied even Santa Claus himself,—shrieks of joy, dances of delight, laughter and tears (for some tender little things could not bear so much pleasure at once, and sobbed with mouths full of candy and hands full of toys). How they ran to show one another the new treasures! how they peeped and tasted, pulled and pinched, until the air was full of queer noises, the floor covered with papers, and the little trees left bare of all but candles!

"I don't think heaven can be any gooder than this," sighed one small girl, as she looked about her in a blissful maze, holding her full apron with one hand, while she luxuriously carried sugar-plums to her mouth with the other.

"Is that a truly angel up there?" asked another, fascinated by the little white figure with the wreath on its shining hair, who in some mysterious way had been the cause of all this merry-making.

"I wish I dared to go and kiss her for this splendid party," said a lame child, leaning on her crutch, as she stood near the steps, wondering how it seemed to sit in a mother's lap, as Effie was doing, while she watched the happy scene before her.

Effie heard her, and remembering Tiny Tim, ran down and put her arms about the pale child, kissing the wistful face, as she said sweetly, "You may; but mamma deserves the thanks. She did it all; I only dreamed about it."

Lame Katy felt as if "a truly angel" was embracing her, and could only stammer out her thanks, while the other children ran to see the pretty spirit, and touch her soft dress, until she stood in a crowd of blue gowns laughing as they held up their gifts for her to see and admire.

Mamma leaned down and whispered one word to the older girls; and suddenly they all took hands to dance round Effie, singing as they skipped.

It was a pretty sight, and the ladies found it hard to break up the happy revel; but it was late for small people, and too much fun is a mistake. So the girls fell into line, and marched before Effie and mamma again, to say goodnight with such grateful little faces that the eyes of those who looked grew dim with tears. Mamma kissed every one; and many a hungry childish heart felt as if the touch of those tender lips was their best gift. Effie shook so many small hands that her own tingled; and when Katy came she pressed a small doll into Effie's hand, whispering, "You didn't have a single present, and we had lots. Do keep that; it's the prettiest thing I got."

"I will," answered Effie, and held it fast until the last smiling face was gone, the surprise all over, and she safe in her own bed, too tired and happy for anything but sleep.

"Mamma, it was a beautiful surprise, and I thank you so much! I don't see how you did it; but I like it best of all the Christmases I ever had, and mean to make one every year. I had my splendid big present, and here is the dear little one to keep for love of poor Katy; so even that part of my wish came true."

And Effie fell asleep with a happy smile on her lips, her one humble gift still in her hand, and a new love for Christmas in her heart that never changed through a long life spent in doing good.

THE GREAT AMERICAN CHRISTMAS DINNER
by Ariel Berkower

MENU

Goose with Apple Stuffing

Roast Turkey with Giblet Gravy

Cranberry Walnut Bread

Fruited Holiday Wreath

Maple Syrup Sweet Potatoes

Classic Cranberry Sauce

Bûche de Noël

Banana Fruitcake

Pumpkin Pie

Lemon Pie

French Chocolate Pie

Apple Cranberry Crumble

Baklava

Eggnog

Punch

Hot Buttered Rum

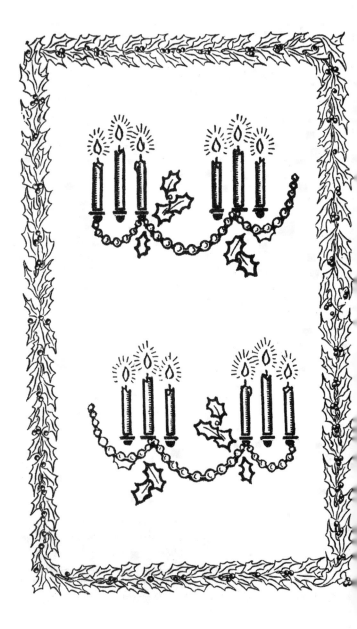

Goose with Apple Stuffing

A traditional favorite, this Christmas goose is sure to bring elegance to your table—and joy to your guests!

SERVES 10-12.

1 cleaned 10- to 12-pound goose, including giblets
2 tablespoons butter
1½ cups chopped apple
¾ cup chopped onion
½ teaspoon instant chicken bouillon granules
½ cup boiling water
4 cups soft bread cubes
1 cup raisins
½ cup chopped almonds
¼ cup snipped parsley
1 teaspoon crushed marjoram
1 teaspoon salt
Pepper, to taste

1. Preheat oven to 375°.
2. Finely chop the goose liver. Heat the butter in a small skillet. Add the liver and cook until tender.
3. Put the apple and onion in a saucepan and cover with water; simmer, covered, until they are tender. Drain.
4. Add the boiling water to the bouillon granules and mix until they are dissolved. Add the apple mixture, liver, bread cubes, raisins, almonds, parsley, marjoram, salt, and pepper, and toss to combine.
5. Rinse the goose and pat it dry with a paper towel. Pull the neck skin back. (You can secure it with a small skewer.) Lightly spoon the stuffing into the goose cavity (do not pack). Tie the legs to the tail and twist the wing tips under the bird. Place it on a rack in a shallow roasting pan. Roast, uncovered, for 3¼ to 3¾ hours or until a meat thermometer registers 185°.
6. Remove stuffing from goose. Carve and serve.

Roast Turkey with Giblet Gravy

The richness of the stuffing and the gravy offsets the leanness of the meat. This recipe is also wonderful at Thanksgiving.

SERVES 12.

14 ounces bread cubes or 1 bag packaged stuffing

¼ cup Italian parsley, minced

2 onions, minced

2 sticks celery, chopped

1 cup chopped walnuts or chestnuts

1 cleaned 14-pound turkey, including giblets

1 stick (4 ounces) butter

2 lemons

5 cups chicken stock

1 tablespoon white flour

1 teaspoon cornstarch

1. Preheat oven to 450°.

2. If you are using packaged stuffing, prepare it according to the package instructions. Add parsley, onions, celery, and nuts to the prepared stuffing or bread cubes.

3. Wash and dry the gizzard, liver, neck, and other giblets. Rub the turkey cavity and the skin with the lemons.

4. Thinly slice a stick of butter and place butter pats all over the turkey skin. Spoon the stuffing into the turkey cavity.

5. Put the turkey into a turkey pan and pour the chicken stock over it. Put it in the oven for 20 minutes.

6. Turn the heat down to 375°. Baste the bird every 15 minutes for just under 5 hours (figure around 20 min-

utes per pound). If it gets too brown, cover it loosely with aluminum foil.

7.   Remove the turkey and set aside for 20 minutes. Meanwhile, skim the fat from the liquid in the pan. Pour ? cup of the drippings into a dish and mix with the flour and the cornstarch until smooth. Return to the pan and stir until thickened.

8.   Remove stuffing from turkey. Carve turkey and serve.

Cranberry Walnut Bread

This sweet, festive bread offers a sparkling alternative to bland white rolls.

SERVES 8-12.

4 cups white flour
1 tablespoon baking powder
1 teaspoon baking soda
¾ teaspoon cinnamon
1½ cup packed brown sugar
½ cup granulated sugar
1 stick (½ cup) butter, melted
1 tablespoon grated orange rind
1½ cups orange juice
2 eggs
2 cups fresh cranberries, chopped
1 cup dried cranberries, chopped
1 cup walnuts, chopped

1.   Preheat oven to 350°. Butter and flour two 9" x 5" bread pans.

2.   Combine all dry ingredients. In a separate bowl, mix the butter, sugar, orange rind, juice, and eggs. Slowly beat in the dry ingredients. Stir in the nuts and the cranberries.

3.   Divide batter evenly between two pans. Bake for 55-60 minutes or until a fork inserted into the center comes out clean.

4.   Cool in the pan for at least ten minutes and turn out.

Fruited Holiday Wreath

Here is the mother of all jello rings. This red, white, and green behemoth is not for amateurs!

SERVES 12-14.

1 8-ounce package cream cheese, softened
¼ cup chopped walnuts
1 3-ounce package lime-flavored gelatin
2 cups boiling water
2½ cups cold water
½ cup chopped celery
1 envelope unflavored gelatin
1 6-ounce can frozen lemonade concentrate, thawed
¼ cup sugar
1 cup mayonnaise or salad dressing
1 16-ounce can fruit cocktail
1 3-ounce package cherry-flavored gelatin
½ cup whipping cream

1.   Dissolve lime-flavored gelatin in 1 cup boiling water and stir in the celery and 1 cup cold water. Chill lime mixture until it is partially set, approximately the consistency of an unbeaten egg white. Pour a little of the lime mixture into an 8½-inch fluted tube pan or a 9½-cup ring mold and chill.

2.   Meanwhile, form cream cheese into 7 balls and roll the balls in walnuts.

3.   When the small amount of lime mixture is almost set, arrange the cream cheese balls in the mold. Slowly pour the remaining lime mixture over the cheese balls, taking care not to disturb the arrangement. Chill.

4.   Meanwhile, soften the unflavored gelatin in ½ cup of cold water, stirring over low heat until the gelatin dissolves. Add ½ cup lemonade concentrate, the sugar, and

the remaining 1 cup of cold water. Add the mayonnaise or salad dressing and chill.

5.   When the lime gelatin is just firm and the lemonade mixture is partially set, pour the lemonade mixture into the mold, taking care not to disturb the green layer. Chill again until almost firm.

6.   Meanwhile, drain the fruit cocktail and reserve the syrup. Add enough water to the syrup to make 1 cup. Dissolve the cherry gelatin in the remaining 1 cup of boiling water and stir in the syrup mixture. Chill.

7.   When the cherry gelatin is partially set, fold the fruit cocktail into it. Carefully pour this mixture over the lemonade layer. Chill the mold until it is firm.

8.   Remove the wreath from its mold.

9.   Combine the remaining mayonnaise with the remaining lemonade concentrate. Whip the cream until it holds soft peaks and fold it into the mayonnaise mixture. Serve alongside the wreath.

Maple Syrup Sweet Potatoes

Sweet, smooth, and delicious.

SERVES 6-8.

4 sweet potatoes, peeled and quartered
4 tablespoons heavy cream
8 tablespoons maple syrup
4 tablespoons butter
Nutmeg, cinnamon, salt, and freshly ground pepper to taste

1.   Place potatoes in a pot of lightly salted cold water and cover.
2.   Bring to a boil. Boil potatoes for 20 minutes.
3.   Drain potatoes and mash them.
4.   Put mashed potatoes in a pot over medium heat. Stir in cream, butter, and maple syrup and mix until creamy.
5.   Stir in seasonings to taste.

Classic Cranberry Sauce

Throw out that jiggly canned goop! Try our Classic Cranberry Sauce—you'll never go back.

SERVES 6-10.

4 cups fresh cranberries
2 cups sugar
1 cup water

1. Combine ingredients in a pot over low heat and cover. Cook for about 15 minutes or until cranberries have burst.
2. Cool completely before serving.

Bûche de Noël

This cake, which resembles a Yule log, is the traditional ending to Christmas dinner in France.

SERVES 12.

WHIPPED CREAM FILLING:
2 cups heavy cream
½ cup confectioners' sugar
1 teaspoon vanilla extract

CAKE:
6 eggs, separated
½ cup sugar
⅓ cup unsweetened cocoa powder
1½ teaspoons vanilla
⅛ teaspoon salt
¼ cup white sugar
Confectioners' sugar for dusting

ICING:
2 ounces unsweetened chocolate
2 tablespoons butter
¼ cup espresso, heated
2 cups confectioners' sugar
1 teaspoon cinnamon

1.   Preheat oven to 375°. Line a 10" x 15" jellyroll pan with parchment paper.

2.   Prepare the whipped cream filling: in a large bowl, whip the cream with the confectioners' sugar and the vanilla until stiff peaks form. Refrigerate.

3.   In a large bowl, beat the egg yolks and the sugar with an electric mixer until thick and pale. Add the cocoa, the vanilla, and the salt.

4.   In a separate bowl, beat the egg whites until soft peaks form. Slowly add the sugar and beat until stiff peaks form. Immediately add the yolk mixture. Spread batter evenly into the jellyroll pan.

5.   Bake for approximately 15 minutes, or until the cake springs back when lightly touched. Remove from oven and let sit for five minutes.

6.   Dust a clean kitchen towel with confectioners' sugar and turn the warm cake onto the towel. Discard the parchment. Roll the cake up in the towel, starting at the shorter end. Set aside to cool.

7.   Unroll cake and spread with whipped cream to within 1 inch of the edge. Re-roll cake with filling inside.

8.   Make the icing: melt the chocolate and the butter together, mixing well. Add the espresso and mix in the sugar and the cinnamon.

9.   Spread the sides and ends of the cake "log" with the chocolate icing, swirling the knife to give the appearance of bark.

Banana Fruitcake

Whether you eat it, gift it, or use it as a doorstop, this fruitcake's for you.

Serves 20.

3 cups (1 16-ounce package) pitted prunes
1½ cups (1 8-ounce package) dried apricots
3 cups (1 15-ounce package) raisins
2 cups (1 16-ounce package) diced mixed candied
     fruits and peels
1⅓ cups (1 8-ounce package) chopped pitted dates
1 cup brandy, plus extra for soaking
1½ cups butter, softened
2 cups packed brown sugar
6 eggs
3 cups all-purpose flour
2 teaspoons salt
1 tablespoon ground cinnamon
1 teaspoon ground nutmeg
1 teaspoon ground allspice
2 large ripe bananas, mashed
2 cups walnut halves

1. Cut prunes and apricots into quarters.
2. Put the dried fruits in a bowl and pour ? cup brandy over them. Cover and let stand overnight.
3. In a large bowl, cream the butter with the brown sugar until fluffy. Add the eggs one by one, beating well after each.
4. In a separate bowl, stir together the flour, salt, and spices. Add the flour mixture and the banana alternately to the butter mixture. Stir in the nuts and the fruit.
5. You should have 15 cups of batter. You may divide the batter into differently sized pans as follows:

Size of Pan	Cups of Batter per Pan	Baking Time (Hours)
9 x 5 x 3-inch	4	3
7½ x 3½ x 2-inch	3	2
4½ x 2½ x 1½-inch	2	2

Grease the pans well before adding the batter.

6. Bake in a 250° oven for the time indicated above or until the cakes look golden. Cool for 10 minutes. Remove from pans and cool completely on racks.

7. Pour ½ cup brandy over the cakes. Wrap them in brandy-soaked cheesecloth; over-wrap with foil. Store in the refrigerator, occasionally adding additional brandy to soak the cakes.

Pie Dough

It wouldn't be Christmas without pie! Employ and enjoy this crust in any of our pie recipes.

FOR A SINGLE-CRUST PIE:
1¼ cups all-purpose flour
½ teaspoon salt
⅓ cup shortening
3-4 tablespoons cold water

FOR A DOUBLE-CRUST PIE:
2 cups all-purpose flour
1 teaspoon salt
⅔ cup shortening
6-7 tablespoons cold water

1.   Stir together the flour and the salt in a medium-sized mixing bowl. Cut in shortening until the pieces are the size of small peas.

2.   Sprinkle 1 tablespoon of water over the flour. Use your hands to blend the water into the dough, adding more water by the tablespoon until all the flour is incorporated.

3.   If you are making a single-crust pie, form the dough into one ball; for a double-crust pie, make two balls.

Pumpkin Pie

SERVES 8-10.

Pie Dough for a Single-Crust Pie (see recipe p. 109)
1 16-ounce can pure pumpkin
¾ cup sugar
1 teaspoon ground cinnamon
½ teaspoon salt
½ teaspoon ground ginger
½ teaspoon ground nutmeg
3 eggs
½ cup milk
⅔ cup (1 5⅓-ounce can) evaporated milk

1.   Roll out the pie dough and line a 9-inch pie plate with it, trimming the pastry to ¼ inch beyond the edge of the pie plate. Flute the edge.

2.   In a large mixing bowl, combine the pumpkin, sugar, cinnamon, salt, ginger, and nutmeg.

3.   Beat the eggs into the pumpkin mixture. Add the milk and the evaporated milk and mix well.

4.   Pour the pumpkin mixture into the crust. Bake at 375° for 50 minutes or until a toothpick inserted into the pumpkin comes out clean.

5.   Cool on a rack before serving. Cover and store leftovers in the refrigerator.

Lemon Pie

SERVES 8-10.

Pie Dough for a Single-Crust Pie (see recipe p. 109)
5 eggs
1½ cups sugar
1 cup light cream
¼ cup butter, melted
1 teaspoon lemon zest
2 tablespoons lemon juice
1 tablespoon all-purpose flour
1 tablespoon yellow cornmeal
1½ teaspoons vanilla

1.   Roll out the pie dough and line a 9-inch pie plate with it. Trim the pastry to ½ inch beyond the edge of the pie plate, and flute the edge. Bake the pie crust at 450° for 5 minutes. Cool on rack.

2.   Beat the eggs until well blended. Add the other ingredients and mix well.

3.   Pour the filling into the partially baked pie shell. Bake at 350° for 40 minutes or until a toothpick inserted into the lemon filling comes out clean.

4.   Cool the pie on a rack before serving. If there are leftovers, cover them and store in the refrigerator.

French Chocolate Pie

SERVES 8-10.

Pie Dough for a Single-Crust Pie (see recipe p. 109)
¾ cup butter
1 cup sugar
3 squares (3 ounces) unsweetened chocolate,
    melted and cooled
1½ teaspoons vanilla
3 eggs

1.   Roll out the pie dough and line a 9-inch pie plate with it. Trim the pastry to ½ inch beyond the edge of the pie plate and flute the edge. Bake the crust at 450° for 10 to 12 minutes. Cool on rack.

2.   In a small mixer bowl, cream the butter with the sugar for about 4 minutes or until light. Mix in the chocolate and the vanilla.

3.   Add the eggs one by one, beating on medium speed (if you are using an electric mixer) for 2 minutes after each addition; at the same time, scrape the sides of the bowl constantly.

4.   Pour the filling into the prepared pie crust.

5.   Chill the pie overnight. If there are leftovers, cover and chill them.

Apple Cranberry Crumble

This recipe is also divine when you substitute nectarines or plums for the apples.

SERVES 8-10.

FILLING:
7 Granny Smith apples, cored and cut into slices
Juice from 2 lemons
2 cups fresh or frozen cranberries
½ cup white sugar

CRUMBLE:
1 cup oats
1½ cups brown sugar
½ cup white flour
½ cup chopped walnuts
1 teaspoon cinnamon
½ teaspoon nutmeg
½ cup (1 stick) butter

1. Preheat oven to 375°.
2. Mix the apples, lemon juice, cranberries, and white sugar. Pour the apple mixture into a 10" x 15" dish.
3. Mix the crumble ingredients in a large bowl, slicing the butter in as you go. Spread the crumble over the filling.
4. Cover the pan with aluminum foil and bake for 30 minutes. Uncover, and bake for another 30 minutes. Let cool for 15 minutes before serving.

Baklava

Unless you have Greek grandparents, this recipe probably never appeared at the Christmases of your childhood. Taste this baklava, and you'll make it a new tradition.

MAKES APPROXIMATELY 50 PIECES.

16 ounces filo dough (21 16 x 12-inch sheets), thawed
1½ cups butter, melted
4 cups walnuts, finely chopped
3 cups pecans, finely chopped
2¾ cup sugar
1 tablespoon cinnamon
1 cup water
2 tablespoons honey
2 tablespoons lemon juice
4 cinnamon sticks

1.   Cut the filo dough to fit your baking pan. If you are using a 13x19x2-inch pan, cut 16x12-inch sheets in half crosswise. Cover with a slightly damp towel.

2.   Butter the bottom of the pan. Layer nine sheets of filo in the pan, brushing each sheet with melted butter as you go.

3.   Mix the walnuts and pecans with the cinnamon and ¾ cup sugar. Sprinkle about 1 cup of the nut mixture over the filo in the pan and drizzle with more melted butter.

4.   Layer four more sheets of filo over the nut mixture, brushing each sheet with more butter. Spread 1 cup of nuts over the four sheets of filo. Pile 5 more of these layers (4 sheets of filo and 1 cup of nuts) into the pan. When you make the fifth layer, use all the remaining nuts and top with nine sheets of filo interspersed with butter.

5.   Cut the baklava into diamonds or squares, cutting to but not through the bottom layer. Bake at 325° for 1 hour. When you take the baklava out of the oven, finish cutting the diamonds or squares and cool.

6.   Meanwhile, combine 2 cups of sugar, the water, the honey, the lemon juice, and the stick cinnamon in a saucepan. Boil gently, uncovered, for 15 minutes, then remove from heat. Remove the cinnamon and stir.

7.   Pour the warm syrup over the cooled pastry. Cool completely before serving.

Eggnog

The ice cream in this recipe makes it extra-luxurious; it's a good after-dinner drink. Don't skimp on the cream; Christmas comes but once a year!

SERVES 8-10.

4 eggs, separated
¼ cup sugar
½ cup bourbon
¼ cup dark rum
1 quart French vanilla ice cream, softened
1 cup whole milk
1 cup heavy cream
Nutmeg

1.   Beat the egg yolks with the sugar until they are a creamy yellow. Stir in the liquor, the ice cream, and the milk. Put the mixture in the freezer.

2.   After dinner, whip the cream with the egg whites. Fold the whipped cream into the yolk mixture, thinning with more milk if necessary.

3.   Spoon the eggnog into cups and sprinkle with nutmeg.

Punch

This alcohol-free punch is great for kids… and your rowdier relatives.

SERVES 4-6.

1 quart apple cider
¼ cup brown sugar
Whole cloves
Allspice buds
1 cinnamon stick
Raisins

1.   Heat the cider in a large pot. Stir in the brown sugar.
2.   Add the spices and the raisins.
3.   Cover the pot. When the punch boils, reduce heat to low and simmer for 15 minutes. Discard the spices.
4.   Serve the punch with a few raisins in each mug.

Hot Buttered Rum

A classic.

SERVES 1

2 dashes bitters
3 ounces dark rum
1 teaspoon butter
Boiling water
3-4 whole cloves

1.   Pour the bitters and the rum into a mug and add the butter. Fill the mug the rest of the way with boiling water.

2.   Stir in the cloves and steep for a few minutes.

3.   Remove the cloves and serve.

GREAT AMERICAN CHRISTMAS COOKIES AND OTHER GOODIES

by Ariel Berkower

*Christmas Sugar Cookies
with Decorating Frosting*

Gingerbread Cookies

Cookie Puzzle

Shortbread

Chocolate-Dipped Chestnut Cookies

Refrigerator Cookies

Candy Cane Cookies

Homemade Marshmallow Snowmen

Cinnamon Bun Christmas Tree

Candy Canes

Lollipops

Caramel Fudge

Hot Chocolate with Peppermint Sticks

Christmas Sugar Cookies with Decorating Frosting

These are the classic Christmas cookies, the ones you remember from when you were small. Get some kids together for a cookie-decorating party.

MAKES 35 TO 60 COOKIES,
DEPENDING ON SIZE.

COOKIES
1 cup (2 sticks) butter at room temperature
1 cup sugar
2 eggs
1 teaspoon vanilla extract
3 cups flour

FROSTING
1 pound confectioners' sugar
3 egg whites
1 tablespoon white vinegar
1 teaspoon vanilla
Food coloring

1.   Cream the butter with the sugar. Beat in the eggs. Stir in the vanilla and the flour. Refrigerate the dough for at least 2 hours.

2.   Preheat the oven to 375°. Line baking sheets with parchment paper.

3.   Roll the dough out on a lightly floured surface and cut with a cookie cutter. Use a spatula to transfer the cookies to the baking sheets.

4.   Put the cookie sheets in the oven for 10 minutes, until the cookies start to brown. Take them out of the oven and slide the parchment off the baking sheet. When the

cookies have cooled somewhat, take them off the parchment to cool further.

5. Meanwhile, make the frosting: beat the egg whites lightly with a fork. Put the confectioners' sugar in a mixing bowl and add the egg whites. Beat for 1 minute with an electric mixer on its lowest speed. Add the vinegar and beat for 2 more minutes at high speed or until the frosting is stiff and glossy.

6. Separate the frosting into several dishes and tint with different colors. You may frost the cookies once they have cooled completely.

Gingerbread Cookies

This dough makes a terrific base for gingerbread men, gingerbread women, gingerbread children, gingerbread pets, gingerbread dinosaurs . . .

MAKES 25-50 COOKIES

7 cups white flour

3 teaspoons baking soda

4 teaspoons ground cinnamon

2 teaspoons ground cloves

4 teaspoons ground ginger

1 cup (2 sticks) butter at room temperature

1 cup white sugar

1 cup brown sugar

1 cup dark corn syrup

1¼ cups heavy cream

1.   Mix together the flour, the baking soda, and the spices.

2.   In a separate bowl, cream the butter with the sugar. Stir in the corn syrup and the cream. Add the dry ingredients little by little and mix well.

3.   Flour your hands and toss the dough briefly on a floured surface. Roll it into three even balls. Cover them with waxed paper and chill for at least 2 hours.

4.   When you are ready to cut the cookies, preheat the oven to 350° and line baking sheets with parchment paper.

5.   Place the dough balls on a lightly floured surface and roll them out one by one. Cut with cookie cutters, using a spatula to transplant them onto the baking sheets.

6.   Bake for 15 to 20 minutes or until the cookies start to turn brown. Remove the sheets from the oven and slide the parchment paper off them. When the cookies have cooled somewhat, remove them from the parchment to cool completely.

❄️

Cookie Puzzle

This whimsical puzzle is a fun twist on the preceding recipes. It makes a terrific edible gift. Try distributing Cookie Puzzles as favors at your Christmas party!

MAKES 1 PUZZLE

1 batch of Christmas Sugar Cookie or Gingerbread Cookie dough

1. Roll the dough into a rectangle.
2. Use a sharp knife to cut the dough in puzzle shapes.
3. Bake the cookies as directed in the original recipe.

Shortbread

Send some shortbread to your far-flung friends—in a sealed container, it will keep for weeks!

MAKES 32 COOKIES

1 cup (2 sticks) butter, softened
¼ cup brown sugar
¼ cup white sugar
1 tablespoon lemon or orange zest
2 cups flour

1.   Preheat oven to 275°. Cut parchment paper to fit two 8" layer cake pans. Butter the pans and line with the parchment. Set aside.

2.   Cream the butter with the sugar in a mixing bowl. Add the zest. Mix in the flour bit by bit until it is completely incorporated and the dough is firm but slightly sticky.

3.   Divide the dough in half and form each half into a ball. Press each ball into a cake pan, smoothing the surface with a spatula until the depth is even.

4.   Press the tines of a fork along the outside edge of the dough to make a design.

5.   Bake the cookies for 35 to 45 minutes, until the cookies are golden but not browned.

6.   Take the cookies out of the oven and cool for ten minutes. Gently turn the shortbread out of the pan. While it is still warm, you can slice the shortbread into wedges with a serrated knife. You can also leave it intact to give it as a gift.

❄️

Chocolate-Dipped Chestnut Cookies

Sweet and nutty—like your relatives.

MAKES 30 COOKIES

¾ cup butter, softened
¼ cup sugar, plus extra for dipping
1 egg yolk
½ cup chestnut purée or canned chestnuts, drained and puréed
¼ teaspoon vanilla
1 cup all-purpose flour
¼ teaspoon salt
¼ teaspoon ground cinnamon
1 egg white, lightly beaten
½ cup semisweet chocolate pieces, melted

1.   In a mixer bowl, cream the butter with ¼ cup sugar. Add the egg yolk and beat until fluffy. Beat in the chestnut purée and vanilla.

2.   In a separate bowl, mix together the flour, the salt, and the cinnamon. Stir the dry ingredients into the chestnut mixture.

3.   Using a tablespoon of dough for each cookie, roll the dough into 2½-inch logs. Dip one side of each cookie into the egg white and then the sugar.

4.   Place the cookies, sugar side up, on a greased cookie sheet and bake at 350° for 20 minutes. Cool the cookies on a rack.

5.   When they are completely cool, dip one end of each cookie in melted chocolate. Put the cookies on waxed paper until the chocolate sets.

Refrigerator Cookies

You can use this basic recipe to make cookies in several different shapes. They are lovely and delicious.

MAKES 35 COOKIES

2 cups (4 sticks) unsalted butter, at room temperature

½ cup sugar

2 teaspoons vanilla extract

2½ cups all purpose white flour

2 tablespoons cocoa

1. Mix the butter with the sugar until it is fluffy. Stir in the vanilla and the flour. Flour your hands and roll the dough into a ball.

2. Divide the dough in half. Blend the cocoa into one half. Wrap each half in plastic wrap or waxed paper and refrigerate for at least 2 hours. At this point, you are ready to prepare any of the following variations.

CHECKERBOARD COOKIES:

1. Use your fingers to shape each ball of dough into two ½-inch-thick, foot-long rolls. Place a cocoa roll next to a white roll. To create the checkerboard effect, put the other cocoa roll on top of the white roll and the other white roll on top of the first cocoa roll.

2. Wrap the whole thing in plastic wrap or waxed paper and return it to the refrigerator. Chill again for at least 1 hour.

3. When you are ready to bake, preheat the oven to 375° and line a baking sheet with parchment paper.

4. Trim the ends of the cookie "log" and cut it into ¼-inch-thick slices. Bake the cookies for 12 to 15 minutes.

CIRCLE COOKIES

1. Divide each ball of dough in half. Take one of the white pieces and one of the cocoa pieces and put each of them between two sheets of parchment. Roll these pieces into 7 x 12-inch rectangles. Put the rectangles, still in their parchment, on baking sheets. Return them to the refrigerator and chill again for at least an hour.

2. Take the remaining sections of white and cocoa dough and divide each into two pieces, one twice the size of the other. Take the bigger pieces and put them between two sheets of parchment. Roll them out into 4½ x 12-inch rectangles. Without removing the parchment, put these rectangles on baking sheets and return them to the refrigerator; chill again for at least an hour.

3. You should be left with two small pieces of dough, one white and one cocoa. Roll each one into a 12-inch log. Wrap it in waxed paper and refrigerate it. Chill again for at least an hour.

4. Once all the dough is thoroughly chilled, remove the top sheet of parchment from the rectangular pieces of dough. Unwrap the white log and place it in the middle of the smaller cocoa rectangle; wrap the cocoa rectangle around it. Repeat with the cocoa log and the smaller white rectangle. Wrap each of the resulting logs in the large rectangle of contrasting color. Finally, re-wrap the logs in parchment or waxed paper and return them to the refrigerator.

5. When you are ready to bake, preheat the oven to 375° and line a baking sheet with parchment paper. Trim the ends of the dough logs and cut them into ¼-inch-thick slices. Bake the cookies for 12 to 15 minutes.

Striped Cookies

1. Divide each ball of dough in halves. Place the four pieces of dough between two sheets of parchment paper and roll them into 3½ x 12-inch rectangles. Put the flattened dough, still in its parchment paper, on baking sheets and return them to the refrigerator. Chill again for at least an hour.

2. Take the dough from the fridge and remove the top pieces of parchment. Layer the rectangles, alternating between cocoa and white dough (remove the parchment as you go). You should finish with a rectangular block of dough. Cover it with waxed paper and chill for another hour.

3. When you are ready to bake, preheat the oven to 375° and line baking sheet with parchment. Trim the ends of the dough block and cut it into slices of ¼" thickness. Place the cookies on the sheet and bake for 12 to 15 minutes.

Candy Cane Cookies

These cookies are irresistibly cute—give them as gifts!

MAKES 30 COOKIES

¾ cup butter, softened
¾ cup sugar
1 egg
½ teaspoon vanilla
½ teaspoon peppermint extract
2 cups all-purpose flour
½ teaspoon salt
¼ teaspoon baking powder
⅓ cup flaked coconut
1 teaspoon red food coloring

1.   In a mixing bowl, cream the butter with the sugar. Beat in the egg, the vanilla, and the peppermint extract.

2.   In a separate dish, mix the flour, the salt, and the baking powder. Stir the dry ingredients into the butter mixture.

3.   Divide the dough in half. Stir the coconut into one half; stir the food coloring into the other half. Cover each and chill for 30 minutes.

4.   Remove one half of the dough from the refrigerator and divide it into 30 balls. Shape each ball into a 5-inch rope. Return the ropes to the refrigerator and remove the other half of the dough. Divide this half into 30 ropes as well.

5.   For each cookie, pinch together one end of a red rope and one end of a white rope. Twist the ropes together and pinch together the remaining ends.

6.   Place the cookies on an ungreased baking sheet. Curve each one to form a cane shape.

7.   Bake the cookies at 375° for about 10 minutes. Cool them on a wire rack before serving.

Homemade Marshmallow Snowmen

These snowmen are the perfect treat for a winter's day—have them ready when the kids come in from making the real thing outside!

MAKES 8 SNOWMEN

3 packets unflavored gelatin
2 cups white sugar
Pinch of salt
2 cups water
2 teaspoons vanilla
2 teaspoons baking powder
2 cups confectioners' sugar
Shredded coconut for dipping
Melted chocolate for decorating

Mix gelatin, sugar, salt, and water in a saucepan and simmer for 10 minutes. Allow to cool.

Add the vanilla, the baking powder, and the confectioners' sugar. Beat until thick.

Spread the mixture into a buttered 9" x 11" pan and refrigerate for 3 hours.

Cut out eight large marshmallow circles and eight smaller ones. Roll the circles in coconut.

Use toothpicks to attach each small circle to a large one. You can also use toothpicks to draw chocolate eyes, mouths, and buttons on the snowmen.

❄

Cinnamon Bun
Christmas Tree

This sweet treat makes a delightful Christmas breakfast.

DOUGH:
2 packages active dry yeast
1 cup milk, warm
3½ cups flour
½ cup (1 stick) butter
¼ cup white sugar
3 egg yolks
½ cup golden raisins
¼ cup pecan halves
1 grated lemon rind
1 teaspoons melted butter
1 cup sugar mixed with 2 teaspoons cinnamon

HONEY GLAZE:
¼ cup butter
1 cup confectioners' sugar
¼ cup honey

WHITE ICING:
¼ cup confectioners' sugar
1½ tablespoons water

1.   Dissolve the yeast in the warm milk and mix in ½ cup flour. Cover and put in a warm place to rise (about 20 minutes).

2.   Meanwhile, cream the butter with the sugar. Mix in the egg yolks one by one. Gradually add the remaining 3 cups of flour and the raisins, pecans, and lemon rind.

3.   Once the yeast has risen, mix it into the dough. Knead for about 7 minutes until the dough is smooth.

4.   Brush the dough with vegetable oil. Place it in a bowl, cover it with a kitchen towel, and put it in a

warm place. Let it rise to twice its size; it will take about 45 minutes.

5.   Punch down the dough and cover it. Let it rise another 30 to 40 minutes.

6.   Punch the dough down again and divide it in half. Roll each half into a rectangle of 12 by 18 inches. Brush each rectangle with melted butter and sprinkle with the cinnamon-sugar.

7.   Take the longer end of one rectangle and roll it tightly; do so with the second rectangle as well. Place the seam sides down and slice buns of ½-inch thickness.

8.   Place four buns in a row near the edge of the cookie sheet. Place three buns above this row so that they nest between the tops of the buns beneath. Continue with two buns in the third row and one bun in the fourth. This triangle of buns forms the Christmas tree. Place a bun beneath the center of the bottom row for a tree stump. Cover the tree with a kitchen towel and allow to rise for 30 minutes.

9.   Meanwhile, preheat the oven to 350°. Prepare the Honey Glaze by creaming the butter with the confectioners' sugar and the honey. Make the White Icing by combining the confectioners' sugar with the water.

10. Brush the remaining melted butter on the tree. Bake it for 30 minutes or until the dough turns golden. Take it from the oven and let cool for 5 minutes. Spread the Honey Glaze on top of the buns. When they are nearly cool, drizzle White Icing on them.

Candy Canes

The classic holiday candy becomes really special when you make it yourself.

MAKES 6 CANDY CANES

2 cups sugar
½ cup light corn syrup
½ cup water
¼ teaspoon cream of tartar
¾ teaspoon peppermint extract
1 teaspoon red food coloring

1. In a large saucepan with a heavy bottom, mix the first four ingredients.

2. Put a candy thermometer in the saucepan. Cook the candy until the thermometer registers 265°. Remove from heat and add the peppermint extract.

3. Pour half of the candy into another pan and add red food coloring to it. Allow both pans to cool.

4. Meanwhile, grease a cookie sheet and butter your hands. Use a buttered spatula to separate a portion of the white taffy; have another person do the same with the red taffy. Pull and fold the pieces until they are glossy. Roll them each into an 8-inch-long rope. Twist the two ropes together, rolling them carefully to make them stick. Twist the head of the cane.

5. Allow the candy canes to harden on the greased cookie sheet.

Lollipops

Sweeter than candy, on a stick…

MAKES 12 LOLLIPOPS

¾ cup sugar
½ cup light corn syrup
¼ cup butter
Food coloring

1.   Butter a heavy 2-quart saucepan and put the sugar, the corn syrup, and the butter in it. Stir this mixture over medium heat until it boils and the sugar dissolves.

2.   Put a candy thermometer in the pot and continue to cook; do not stir. When the thermometer reads 270°, turn off the heat. Add food coloring and stir.

3.   Arrange 12 wooden skewers 4 inches apart on a buttered baking sheet. To form the pops, drizzle hot syrup from the tip of a tablespoon over the skewers; the candy should be 2 to 3 inches in diameter.

4.   Allow the lollipops to cool before serving.

❄️

Caramel Fudge

Who doesn't love fudge? This is one of the most reliable crowd-pleasers you can make.

MAKES 35 PIECES

¾ cup butter
2 cups packed brown sugar
½ cup evaporated milk
1 teaspoon vanilla
3 cups powdered sugar
1 cup chopped walnuts

1. Melt the butter in a heavy 2-quart saucepan. Add the brown sugar and cook over low heat for 2 minutes, stirring constantly. Add the evaporated milk and stir until the mixture boils. At that point, remove from heat.

2. Cool the mixture until it is lukewarm (a candy thermometer will read 110°). Stir in the vanilla. Add the powdered sugar bit by bit, beating vigorously until the mixture reaches a fudgey consistency (around 2 minutes). Stir in the nuts.

3. Spread the candy in a buttered 8 x 8 x 2-inch pan. Chill it and cut into squares.

Hot Chocolate with Peppermint Sticks and Whipped Cream

This is hot chocolate as it should be.

FOR THE CHOCOLATE
Whole milk
Unsweetened cocoa
White sugar
Peppermint sticks

FOR THE CREAM
½ pint whipping cream
1 teaspoon vanilla extract
1 teaspoon white sugar

1. Following the proportions indicated on the cocoa package, pour the milk and the cocoa into a medium saucepan over low heat.

2. With an egg beater or whisk, whip the mixture until it is smooth.

3. When the chocolate is warm but not boiling, add the sugar.

4. Prepare the Whipped Cream: combine all ingredients in a mixing bowl and whip with an electric mixer or whisk until stiff peaks form.

5. Pour the Hot Chocolate into mugs. Pile Whipped Cream on top and stir with peppermint sticks.

HOME-MADE CANDY

$\mathcal{W}$E have noticed that in none of the books we have seen, which were written especially for the amusement and entertainment of girls, has there been any directions or recipes for making candy. Knowing by experience that most girls consider candy-making one of their prime winter enjoyments, we consider the omission to be quite an important one, and we will in this chapter endeavor to supply the much-wished-for-information.

Though cooking in general may not be regarded with much favor by the average school-girl, she is always anxious to learn how to make candy, and hails a new recipe as a boon.

The following recipes for peanut-candy, butter-scotch, and molasses-candy were obtained from a friend who makes the best homemade candy it has ever been our good-fortune to taste, and as she recommends them, we may rely upon their being excellent. We give them, with her comments, just as she wrote them.

❄

Delicious Peanut-Candy

This is delicious, *and* so *quickly made.*

1.   Shell your peanuts and chop them fine; measure them in a cup, and take just the same quantity of granulated sugar as you have peanuts.

2.   Put the sugar in a skillet, or spider, on the fire, and keep moving the skillet around until the sugar is dissolved.

3.   Put in the peanuts and pour into buttered tins.

Butter-Scotch

2 cups of brown sugar

½ cup of butter

4 tablespoonfuls of molasses

2 tablespoonfuls of water

2 tablespoonfuls of vinegar

1.   Boil until it hardens when dropped into cold water, then pour into buttered tins.

Molasses-Candy

Splendid!

2 cups of brown sugar.
½ cup of New Orleans molasses.
⅔ cup of vinegar and water mixed.
A piece of butter half the size of an egg

1.   When the candy hardens in cold water, pour into shallow buttered tins

2.   As soon as it is cool enough to handle, pull it until it is of a straw-color.

Here are two recipes which another friend has kindly sent us

Chocolate-Creams

1 egg white
cold water
1 lb confectioner's sugar
vanilla, to flavor
chocolate

1.   To the white of 1 egg add an equal quantity of cold water.

2.   Stir in 1 pound of confectioner's sugar.

3.   Flavor with vanilla. Stir until fine and smooth; then mold into balls and drop into melted chocolate.

4.   To melt the chocolate, scrape and put it in a tin-cup or small sauce-pan over a kettle where it will steam. Let the chocolate be melting while the cream is being prepared.

Walnut-Creams

1. Make the cream as for chocolate-drops and mold into larger balls.

2. Place the half of an English walnut on either side and press them into the cream.

3. The cream prepared in this way, we have found, can be used for various kinds of candy.

4. Small pieces of fruit of any kind and nuts can be enclosed in the cream, making a great variety.

5. Chocolate may be mixed with it; and if strong, clear coffee is used in place of the water, the candy will have the coffee flavor and color which some people like.

Walnut and Fruit Glacè

1 cup sugar
½ cold water
1 cup shelled walnuts
whichever fruit you desire

1. Put 1 cup of sugar and ½ cup of water in a saucepan and stir until the sugar is all dissolved; then place it over the fire and let it boil until it hardens and is quite crisp when dropped in cold water. Do not stir it after it is put on the fire.

2. When cooked sufficiently, dip out a spoonful at a time and drop in buttered tins, leaving a space of an inch or so between each spoonful. Place on each piece of candy the half of a walnut, or the fruit which has previously been prepared, and pour over them enough candy to cover them, always keeping each piece separate.

3. Any kind of fruit can be made into glace. When using oranges, quarter them and remove the seeds. Strawberries, in their season, and peaches also make delicious glace.

The remainder of our recipes have been taken from family recipe-books, and although we have not tested them ourselves, we think it may be safely said that they are good ones.

Marsh-mallow Paste

1 lb white gum-arabic
1 lb refined sugar
8 egg whites
1 teaspoon vanilla

1. Dissolve 1 pound of clean white gum-arabic in one quart of water; strain, add 1 pound of refined sugar, and place over the fire.

2. Stir continually until the syrup is dissolved and the mixture has become the consistency of honey.

3. Next add gradually the beaten whites of 8 eggs; stir the mixture all the time until it loses its thickness and does not adhere to the finger.

4. Flavor with vanilla or rose. Pour into a tin slightly dusted with powdered starch, and when cool divide into squares with a sharp knife.

Toasted Marsh-mallows

1. Tie a string on the end of a cane or stick, fasten a bent pin on the end of the string, and stick the pin into a marsh-mallow-drop.

2. Hold the marsh-mallow suspended over an open fire and let it gradually toast.

3. When it begins to melt and run down, it is done.

For a small party toasting marsh-mallows will be found quite a merry pastime, and a great many persons consider the candy much better for being thus cooked the second time.

❄

Molasses Peanut-Candy

2 cups of molasses.
1 cup of brown sugar.
1 tablespoonful of butter.
1 tablespoonful of vinegar.

1.   While the candy is boiling remove the shells and brown skins from the peanuts, lay the nuts in buttered pans, and when the candy is done pour it over them.

2.   While it is still warm cut in blocks.

Chocolate-Caramels

2 cups of sugar.

1 cup of molasses.

1 cup of milk.

1 tablespoonful of butter.

1 tablespoonful of flour.

½ pound of Baker's chocolate.

1. Grease your pot, put in sugar, molasses, and milk.

2. Boil fifteen minutes, and add butter and flour stirred to a cream.

3. Let it boil another five minutes, then add the chocolate, grated, and boil until quite thick.

4. Grease shallow pans and pour in the candy half an inch thick, marking it in squares before it becomes hard.

Pop-Corn Balls

6 quarts of popped corn.
1 pint of molasses.

1. Boil the molasses about fifteen minutes
2. Put the corn into a large pan, pour the molasses over it, and stir briskly until thoroughly mixed.
3. Then, with clean hands, make into balls of the desired size.

CHRISTMAS EDITORIAL

Yes, Virginia, There Is a Santa Claus

FRANCIS P. CHURCH

Dear Editor:
I am 8 years old. Some of my friends say there is no Santa
Claus. Papa says "If you see it in The Sun *it's so." Please*
tell me the truth; is there a Santa Claus?

Virginia O'Hanlon

VIRGINIA, your little friends are wrong. They have been affected by the skepticism of a skeptical age. They do not believe except they see. They think that nothing can be which is not comprehensible by their little minds. All minds, Virginia, whether they be men's or children's, are little. In this great universe of ours man is a mere insect, an ant, in his intellect, as compared with the boundless world about him, as measured by the intelligence capable of grasping the whole of truth and knowledge.

Yes, Virginia, there is a Santa Claus. He exists as certainly as love and generosity and devotion exist, and you know that they abound and give to your life its highest beauty and joy. Alas! how dreary would be the world if there were no Santa Claus! It would be as dreary as if there were no Virginias. There would be no child-like faith then, no poetry, no romance to make tolerable this existence. We should have no enjoyment, except in sense and sight. The eternal light with which childhood fills the world would be extinguished.

Not believe in Santa Claus! You might as well not believe in fairies. You might get your papa to hire men to watch in all the chimneys on Christmas Eve to catch Santa Claus, but even if they did not see Santa Claus coming down, what would that prove? Nobody sees Santa Claus, but that is no sign that there is no Santa Claus. The most real things in the world are those that neither children nor men can see.

No Santa Claus! Thank God, he lives, and he lives forever. A thousand years from now, Virginia, nay, ten times ten thousand years from now, he will continue to make glad the heart of childhood.

—*The New York Sun*,
September 21, 1891

HOW TO SELECT AND CUT A CHRISTMAS TREE
by Marina R. Zhavoronkova

The Christmas tree is the centerpiece of most holiday celebrations. It is the site of gifts, tinsel, and lights, and it is worth some careful consideration. There are several factors to bear in mind before selecting your Christmas tree. What are the measurements of your living room? How heavy is the unfortunate Rudolph-Santa hybrid that your niece crafted—and are the needles thick enough to conceal it from view? How do you prevent the pine allergies that leave you chugging benadryl instead of eggnog? What color do you want your tree—green, white, or fluorescent pink?

I. SELECTION

SIZE—Measure your available space before you make the trip; don't estimate. Your point of reference at home may be your ceiling fan, but the ceiling at the tree lot—the sky—is generally a bit higher. When measuring width, remember to measure the bottom of the tree, since it is trimmed to taper upwards.

SIZE—Hundreds of different species of pine and fir are sold as Christmas trees. Chances are, your local lot will be limited to several popular species: balsam fir, blue spruce, Douglas fir, Fraser fir, Virginia Pine, and Eastern white pine.[1] sugar-free?

• *Balsam Fir*: This tree has long-lasting needles, a pleasant pine fragrance, and compact foliage that supports large ornaments.

• *Blue Spruce*: The blue spruce gets its name from the color of its foliage, which varies from blue to silver, giving the tree a frosty, whimsical appearance. Although this tree is very stiff and spatially ideal for ornaments, beware of its sharp needles.

• *Douglas Fir*: The Douglas is another classic Christmas tree choice. It is dark green and naturally even, pyramid-shaped, and gives off a subtle evergreen fragrance.

• *Fraser Fir*: This species is fragrant with thick, symmetrical branches and dense, two-toned needles. One side is dark blue-green, and the other is a festive silver. Traditional and attractive, this is one of the most popular Christmas firs.

• *Virginia Pine*: Once the staple of the Christmas tree industry, this dark pine has open branching, is useful for larger decorations, and gives off the classic evergreen scent. However, this tree comes with a sticky surprise that may get children into trouble: sap.

• *Eastern White Pine*: This tree is best for smaller ornaments and thin lights. It is cone-shaped, ranges in color from blue-green to silver, and its light fragrance is less of an allergen than other trees.

---

1. Source: National Christmas Tree Association.

There are other, less well-known species that can offer a variation from the norm. The Carolina Sapphire is sprinkled with tiny yellow flowers, and the tree's dense, soft foliage will not be a source of tears for children; for those of us with allergies, the aroma of lemon and mint will be a relief. If you wish to cultivate their own tree but would prefer not to spend ten years doing so, the Leyland Cypress is known for its relatively rapid growth rate.

II. Buying

Next, it's time to find your tree and lug it home. The most popular way of getting a pre-cut tree is at a retail lot, but seeing as you've managed to purchase this book it can be safely assumed that accessing them doesn't need explanation. Tree farms offer a selection of live trees and a complimentary workout: you will be cutting your own trunk. This is not a one person job, and will take up a good portion of your day. Saws are usually provided by the farm operator, but the responsibility for a clean cut is yours.

At retail lots and tree farms, needle retention is the main indicator of your tree's freshness. To test a pine tree, grip a branch and pull it lightly. A few needles should come loose, but avoid a tree that produces a prickly shower. Likewise, a fir tree needle should snap easily when bent.

For the environmentally conscious, a live tree is a friendly option. Consider how well the species you have chosen will adapt to your backyard, and how much care and attention it will require. The most important part of the tree is its root, and it should be kept moist and nourished before its starring role in your living room. The ground is likely to be frozen at this time of year, so after your tree has played its part, replant it in a prepared hole. Reinforce it with a stake, and cover the root area with mulch and burlap.

Of course, there is always another option: artificial trees. They are found in the classic green, but also white, silver, blue, and any other color one could generally find in a pack of highlighters. It may be an easy way out, but it is a cheap, reusable, clean way out as well!

III. Setting Up

If you take care of your tree properly, it should live for at least five weeks. And by "care" we mean water. Water needs to reach the tree through the base, so make sure it has a fresh cut (a trim of at least ? of an inch). This cut can form a seal of sap in six hours, keeping water saturating the rest of the tree, so it is important to set up your tree right away.

The simplest way to ensure your tree has enough water is to purchase a tree stand. On average, a fresh Christmas tree consumes about one gallon of water a day,[2] so a tree stand that can hold one gallon of water should be refilled daily.

Always remember to keep your tree away from fire hazards (furnaces, fireplaces, radiators, wood stoves, etc).

And now we are ready to decorate . . .

---

2. Source: National Christmas Tree Association

CHRISTMAS AT HYDE PARK
by Eleanor Roosevelt

*W*HEN our children were young, we spent nearly every Christmas holiday at Hyde Park. We always had a party the afternoon of Christmas Eve for all the families who lived on the place. The presents were piled under the tree, and after everyone had been greeted, my husband would choose the children old enough to distribute gifts and send them around to the guests. My mother-in-law herself always gave out her envelopes with money, and I would give out ours. The cornucopias filled with old-fashioned sugar candies and the peppermint canes hanging on the trees were distributed, too, and then our guests would leave us and enjoy their ice cream, cake, and coffee or milk in another room. Later in the day, when the guests had departed, my husband would begin the reading of *A Christmas Carol*. He never read it through; but he would select parts he thought suitable for the youngest members of the family. Then, after supper, he would read other parts for the older ones.

On Christmas morning, I would get up and close the windows in our room, where all the stockings had been hung on the mantel. The little children would be put into our bed and given their stockings to open. The others would sit around the fire. I tried to see that they all had a glass of orange juice before the opening of stockings really began, but the excitement was so great I was not always successful.

Breakfast was late Christmas morning, and my husband resented having to go to church on Christmas Day and sometimes flatly refused to attend. But I would go with my mother-in-law and such children as she could persuade to accompany us. For the most part, however, the children stayed home. In later year, I went to midnight service on Christmas Eve, and we gave up going to church in the morning.

I remembered the excitement as each child grew old enough to have his own sled and would start out after breakfast to try it on the hill behind the stable. Franklin would go coasting with them, and until the children were nearly grown, he was the only one who ever piloted the bobsled down the hill. Everyone came in for a late lunch, and at dusk we would light the candles on the tree again. Only outdoor presents like sleds and skates were distributed in the morning. The rest were kept for the late-afternoon Christmas tree. Again they were piled under the tree, and my husband and the children scrambled around it, and the he called the names.

At first, my mother-in-law did a great deal of shopping and wrapping, and the Hyde Park Christmas always included her gifts. Later, she found shopping too difficult. Then she would give each person a check, though she managed very often to give her son the two things she knew he would not buy for himself-silk shirts and silk pajamas. These she bought in London, as a rule, and saved for his Christmas, which to her was always very special.

In the early years of our marriage, I did a great deal more sewing and embroidering than I've done since, so many of my gifts were things I had made. The family still has a few pieces of Italian cutwork embroidery and other kinds of my perfectly useless handwork. I look back, however, with some pleasure on the early Hyde Park days, when I would have a table filled with pieces of silk and make sachets of different scents. I would dry pine needles at Campobello Island and make then into sweet-smelling bags for Christmas. Now I rarely give a present I have made, and perhaps, it is just as well, for what one buys is likely better made!

Each of the children had a special preference in gifts. When Anna was a small child, her favorite present was a rocking horse, on which she spent many hours. Later, she was to spend even more hours training her own horse, which her great-uncle Mr. Warren Delano gave her. One of the nicest gifts we could possibly give her as she grew older was something for her horse, Natomah. Jimmy loved boats from the very beginning, whether he floated them in the bathtub or later competed with his father in the regattas of toy boats on the Hudson River. Elliott was always trying to catch up with his older brother and sister; but because he was delicate as a child, I think he read more than the others. I remember that books and games were very acceptable gifts for him. Franklin, Jr., and John were a pair and had to have pretty much the same things, or they would quarrel over them. They had learned together to ride and to swim, so gifts for outdoor sports were always favorites of theirs.

My children teased me because their stockings inevitably contained toothbrushes, toothpaste, nail cleaners, soap, washcloths, etc. They said Mother never ceased to remind them that cleanliness was next to godliness—even on Christmas morning. In the toe of each stocking, I always put a purse, with a dollar bill for the young ones and a five-dollar bill for the older ones. These bills were hoarded to supplement the rather meager allowances they had. When I was able to buy sucre d'orge (barley sugar), I put that in their stockings, together with some old-fashioned peppermint sticks; but as they grew older, this confection seemed to vanish from the market, and I had to give it up and substitute chocolates. The stockings also contained families of little china pigs or rabbits or horses, which the children placed on their bookshelves.

The children themselves could probably tell much better than I can the things they remember most about these years. But I know that all of them have carried on many of the Hyde Park Christmas traditions with their own children. Today, some of my grandchildren are establishing the same customs, and my great-grandchildren will one day remember the same kind of Christmas we started so many years ago.

CAROLS, CAROLS, AND MORE CAROLS

"Use what talents you have;
the woods would have
little music if no birds
sang their song except those
who sang best."
—Reverend Oliver G. Wilson

Joy to the World!

Joy to the world! The Lord is come;
Let earth receive her King.
Let ev'ry heart prepare Him room,
And heav'n and nature sing,
And heav'n and nature sing,
And heav'n and heaven and nature sing.

Joy to the world! The Savior reigns;
Let men their songs employ,
While fields and floods, rocks, hills, and plains
Repeat the sounding joy,
Repeat the sounding joy,
Repeat, repeat the sounding joy.

He rules the world with truth and grace,
And makes the nations prove
The glories of His righteousness,
And wonders of His love,
And wonders of His love,
And wonders, and wonders, of His love.

O Come, All Ye Faithful

O Come, All Ye Faithful, joyful and triumphant,
O come ye, O come ye, to Bethlehem.
Come and behold Him, born the King of Angels
O come, let us adore Him,
O come, let us adore Him,
O come, let us adore Him,
Christ, the Lord.
Sing, choirs of angels, sing in exultation,
O sing, all ye citizens of heav'n above!
Glory to God, all Glory in the highest;
O come, let us adore Him,
O come, let us adore Him,
O come, let us adore Him,
Christ, the Lord.
Yea, Lord, we greet Thee, born this happy morning,
Jesus, to Thee be all glory giv'n;
Word of the Father, now in flesh appearing;
O come, let us adore Him,
O come, let us adore Him,
O come, let us adore Him,
Christ, the Lord.

Hark! The Herald Angels Sing

Hark! The Herald Angels Sing,
"Glory to the newborn King!
Peace on earth, and mercy mild,
God and sinners reconciled."
Joyful, all ye nations rise;
Join the triumph of the skies;
With th'angelic host proclaim,
"Christ is born in Bethlehem."
Hark! The Herald Angels Sing,
"Glory to the newborn King!"
Christ, by highest heaven adored;
Christ, the everlasting Lord;
Come, Desire of Nations, come,
Fix in us thy humble home.
Veiled in flesh the Godhead see;

Hail th'Incarnate Deity,
Pleased as man with man to dwell,
Jesus, our Emmanuel.
Hark! The Herald Angels Sing,
"Glory to the newborn King!"
Hail, the heaven-born Prince of Peace!
Hail, the Sun of Righteousness!
Light and life to all He brings,
Ris'n with healing in His wing;
Mild He lays His glory by,
Born that man no more may die,
Born to raise the sons of earth,
Born to give them second birth;
Hark! The Herald Angels Sing,
"Glory to the newborn King!"

The Twelve Days of Christmas

On the first day of Christmas my true love gave to me,
A partridge in a pear tree.

On the second day of Christmas my true love gave to me,
Two turtledoves and a partridge in a pear tree.

On the third day of Christmas my true love gave to me,
Three French hens, two turtledoves and a partridge in a
pear tree.

On the fourth day of Christmas my true love gave to me,
Four mockingbirds, three French hens, two turtledoves
and a partridge in a pear tree.

On the fifth day of Christmas my true love gave to me,
Five golden rings, four mockingbirds, three French hens,
two turtledoves and a partridge in a pear tree.

On the sixth day of Christmas my true love gave to me,
Six geese a-laying, five golden rings, four mockingbirds,
three French hens, two turtledoves and a partridge in a
pear tree.

On the seventh day of Christmas my true love gave to me,
Seven swans a-swimming, six geese a-laying, five golden
rings, four mockingbirds, three French hens, two turtledoves and a partridge in a pear tree.

On the eighth day of Christmas my true love gave to me,
Eight maids a-milking, seven swans a-swimming, six geese
a-laying, five golden rings, four mockingbirds, three
French hens, two turtledoves and a partridge in a pear tree.

On the ninth day of Christmas my true love gave to me,
Nine ladies dancing, eight maids a-milking, seven swans a-
swimming, six geese a-laying, five golden rings, four
mockingbirds, three French hens, two turtledoves and a
partridge in a pear tree.

On the tenth day of Christmas my true love gave to me,
Ten lords a-leaping, nine ladies dancing, eight maids a-
milking, seven swans a-swimming, six geese a-laying, five
golden rings, four mockingbirds, three French hens, two
turtledoves and a partridge in a pear tree.

On the eleventh day of Christmas my true love gave to me,
Eleven pipers piping, ten lords a-leaping, nine ladies dancing, eight maids a-milking, seven swans a-swimming, six geese a-laying, five golden rings, four mockingbirds, three French hens, two turtledoves and a partridge in a pear tree.

On the twelfth day of Christmas my true love gave to me,
Twelve drummers drumming, eleven pipers piping, ten lords a-leaping, nine ladies dancing, eight maids a-milking, seven swans a-swimming, six geese a-laying, five golden rings, four mockingbirds, three French hens, two turtledoves and a partridge in a pear tree.

Angels We Have Heard on High

Angels We Have Heard on High,
Sweetly singing o'er the plain,
And the mountains in reply
Echoing their joyous strain.
Gloria, in excelsis Deo!
Gloria, in excelsis Deo!
Shepherds, why this jubilee

Why your joyful strains prolong

What the gladsome tidings be
Which inspire your heav'nly song

Gloria, in excelsis Deo!
Gloria, in excelsis Deo!
Come to Bethlehem and see
Him whose birth the angels sing;
Come adore on bended knee
Christ, the Lord, the new-born King.
Gloria, in excelsis Deo!
Gloria, in excelsis Deo!
See Him in a manger laid,
Whom the choirs of angels praise;
Holy Spirit, lend thine aid,
While our hearts in love we raise.
Gloria, in excelsis Deo!
Gloria, in excelsis Deo!

Deck the Halls

Deck the Halls with boughs of holly,
Fa la la la la la la la la.
'Tis the season to be jolly,
Fa la la la la la la la la.

Don we now our gay apparel,
Fa la la la la la la la la.
Troll the ancient Yuletide carol,
Fa la la la la la la la la.

See the blazing Yule before us,
Fa la la la la la la la la.
Strike the harp and join the chorus,
Fa la la la la la la la la.

Follow me in merry measure,
Fa la la la la, la la la la.
While I tell of Yuletide treasure,
Fa la la la la la la la la.

Fast away the old year passes,
Fa la la la la la la la la.
Hail the new ye lads and lasses,
Fa la la la la la la la la.

Sing we joyous all together,
Fa la la la la la la la la.
Heedless of the wind and weather,
Fa la la la la la la la la.

Silent Night

Silent Night, holy night,
All is calm, all is bright.
'Round yon virgin mother and child.
Holy infant, so tender and mild,
Sleep in heavenly peace,
Sleep in heavenly peace.
Silent night! Holy night!
Shepherds quake at the sight!
Glories stream from Heaven afar,
Heav'nly hosts sing Alleluia!
Christ the Savior is born!
Christ the Savior is born!
Silent night! Holy night!
Son of God, love's pure light,
Radiant beams from Thy holy face,
With the dawn of redeeming grace,
Jesus, Lord, at Thy birth,
Jesus, Lord, at Thy birth.

The Holly and the Ivy

The Holly and the Ivy,
Now both are full well grown,
Of all the trees that are in the wood,
The Holly bears the crown.
Refrain:
O the rising of the sun,
The running of the deer,
The playing of the merry organ,
Sweet singing in the choir,
Sweet singing in the choir.
The Holly bears a blossom
As white as lily flow'r;
And Mary bore sweet Jesus Christ,
To be our sweet Savior.
Refrain
The Holly bears a berry
As red as any blood;
And Mary bore sweet Jesus Christ
To do poor sinners good.
Refrain
The Holly bears a prickle,
As sharp as any thorn,
And Mary bore sweet Jesus Christ
On Christmas Day in the morn.
Refrain
The Holly bears a bark,
As bitter as any gall;
And Mary bore sweet Jesus Christ,
For to redeem us all.
Refrain

O Come, All Ye Faithful

O come, all ye faithful, joyful and triumphant,
O come ye, O come ye, to Bethlehem.
Come and behold Him, born the King of Angels.

Refrain:
O come, let us adore Him,
O come, let us adore Him,
O come, let us adore Him,
Christ, the Lord.

True God of true God, Light from Light Eternal,
Lo, He shuns not the Virgin's womb;
Son of the Father, begotten, not created,

Refrain

Sing, choirs of angels, sing in exultation;
O sing, all ye citizens of heav'n above!
Glory to God, all Glory in the highest,

Refrain

See how the shepherds, summoned to His cradle,
Leaving their flocks, draw nigh to gaze;
We too will thither bend our joyful footsteps;

Refrain

Lo! star led chieftains, Magi, Christ adoring,
Offer Him incense, gold, and myrrh;
We to the Christ Child bring our hearts' oblations.

Refrain

Child, for us sinners poor and in the manger,
We would embrace Thee, with love and awe;
Who would not love Thee, loving us so dearly

Refrain

Yea, Lord, we greet Thee, born this happy morning;
Jesus, to Thee be all glory giv'n;
Word of the Father, Now in flesh appearing,

Refrain

Good King Wenceslas

Good King Wenceslas looked out
On the Feast of Stephen,
When the snow lay 'round about,
Deep and crisp and even.

Brightly shone the moon that night,
Though the frost was cruel,
When a poor man came in sight
Gath'ring winter fuel.

"Hither, page, and stand by me,
If thou know'st it, telling,
Yonder peasant, who is he
Where and what his dwelling"

"Sire, he lives a good league hence,
Underneath the mountain,
Right against the forest fence,
By Saint Agnes's fountain."

"Bring me food and bring me wine,
Bring me pine-logs hither,
Thou and I will see him dine,
When we bear them hither."

Page and monarch, forth they went,
Forth they went together,
Through the rude wind's wild lament
And the bitter weather.

"Sire, the night is darker now,
And the wind blows stronger.
Fails my heart, I know not how;
I can go no longer."

"Mark my footsteps, my good page,
Tread now in them boldly.
Thou shalt find the winter's rage
Freeze your blood less coldly."

In his master's steps he trod,
Where the snow lay dinted;
Heat was in the very sod
Which the saint had printed.

Therefore, Christian men, be sure,
Wealth or rank possessing,
Ye who now will bless the poor,
Shall yourselves find blessing.

Carol of the Bells

Hark how the bells,
Sweet silver bells,
All seem to say
Throw cares away.

Christmas is here,
Bringing good cheer,
To young and old,
Meek and the bold.

Ding dong ding dong,
That is their song.
With joyful ring,
All caroling.

One seems to hear
Words of good cheer
From everywhere
Filling the air.

Oh, how they pound,
Raising the sound
O'er hill and dale,
Telling their tale.

Gaily they ring
While people sing
Songs of good cheer,
Christmas is here.

Merry, merry, merry, merry Christmas.
Merry, merry, merry, merry Christmas.

On, on they send,
On without end,
Their joyful tone
To every home.

Ding dong ding, dong.
Bong!

THE GIFT OF THE MAGI
by O. Henry

ONE dollar and eighty-seven cents. That was all. And sixty cents of it was in pennies. Pennies saved one and two at a time by bulldozing the grocer and the vegetable man and the butcher until one' cheeks burned with the silent imputation of parsimony that such close dealing implied. Three times Della counted it. One dollar and eighty-seven cents. And the next day would be Christmas.

There was clearly nothing to do but flop down on the shabby little couch and howl. So Della did it. Which instigates the moral reflection that life is made up of sobs, sniffles, and smiles, with sniffles predominating.

While the mistress of the home is gradually subsiding from the first stage to the second, take a look at the home. A furnished flat at $8 per week. It did not exactly beggar description, but it certainly had that word on the lookout for the mendicancy squad.

In the vestibule below was a letter-box into which no letter would go, and an electric button from which no mortal finger could coax a ring. Also appertaining thereunto was a card bearing the name "Mr. James Dillingham Young."

The "Dillingham" had been flung to the breeze during a former period of prosperity when its possessor was being paid $30 per week. Now, when the income was shrunk to $20, though, they were thinking seriously of contracting to a modest and unassuming D. But whenever Mr. James Dillingham Young came home and reached his flat above he was called "Jim" and greatly hugged by Mrs. James Dillingham Young, already introduced to you as Della. Which is all very good.

Della finished her cry and attended to her cheeks with the powder rag. She stood by the window and looked out dully at a gray cat walking a gray fence in a gray backyard. Tomorrow would be Christmas Day, and she had only $1.87 with which to buy Jim a present. She had been saving every penny she could for months, with this result. Twenty dollars a week doesn't go far. Expenses had been greater than she had calculated. They always are. Only $1.87 to buy a present for Jim. Her Jim. Many a happy hour she had spent planning for something nice for him. Something fine and rare and sterling—something just a little bit near to being worthy of the honor of being owned by Jim.

There was a pier-glass between the windows of the room. Perhaps you have seen a pier-glass in an $8 flat. A very thin and very agile person may, by observing his reflection in a rapid sequence of longitudinal strips, obtain a fairly accurate conception of his looks. Della, being slender, had mastered the art.

Suddenly she whirled from the window and stood before the glass. Her eyes were shining brilliantly, but her face had lost its color within twenty seconds. Rapidly she pulled down her hair and let it fall to its full length.

Now, there were two possessions of the James Dillingham Youngs in which they both took a mighty pride. One was Jim's gold watch that had been his father's and his grandfather's. The other was Della's hair. Had the queen of Sheba lived in the flat across the airshaft, Della would have let her hair hang out the window some day to dry just to depreciate Her Majesty's jewels and gifts. Had King Solomon been the janitor, with all his treasures piled up in the basement, Jim would have pulled out his watch every time he passed, just to see him pluck at his beard from envy.

So now Della's beautiful hair fell about her rippling and shining like a cascade of brown waters. It reached below her knee and made itself almost a garment for her. And then she did it up again nervously and quickly. Once she faltered for a minute and stood still while a tear or two splashed on the worn red carpet.

On went her old brown jacket; on went her old brown hat. With a whirl of skirts and with the brilliant sparkle still in her eyes, she fluttered out the door and down the stairs to the street.

Where she stopped the sign read: "Mne. Sofronie. Hair Goods of All Kinds." One flight up Della ran, and collected herself, panting. Madame, large, too white, chilly, hardly looked the "Sofronie."

"Will you buy my hair?" asked Della.

"I buy hair," said Madame. "Take yer hat off and let's have a sight at the looks of it."

Down rippled the brown cascade.

"Twenty dollars," said Madame, lifting the mass with a practiced hand.

"Give it to me quick," said Della.

Oh, and the next two hours tripped by on rosy wings. Forget the hashed metaphor. She was ransacking the stores for Jim's present.

She found it at last. It surely had been made for Jim and no one else. There was no other like it in any of the stores, and she had turned all of them inside out. It was a platinum fob chain simple and chaste in design, properly proclaiming its value by substance alone and not by meretricious ornamentation—as all good things should do. It was even worthy of The Watch. As soon as she saw it she knew that it must be Jim's. It was like him. Quietness and value—the description applied to both. Twenty-one dollars they took from her for it, and she hurried home with the 87 cents. With that chain on his watch Jim might be properly anxious about the time in any company. Grand as the watch was, he sometimes looked at it on the sly on account of the old leather strap that he used in place of a chain.

When Della reached home her intoxication gave way a little to prudence and reason. She got out her curling irons and lighted the gas and went to work repairing the ravages made by generosity added to love. Which is always a tremendous task, dear friends—a mammoth task.

Within forty minutes her head was covered with tiny, close-lying curls that made her look wonderfully like a truant schoolboy. She looked at her reflection in the mirror long, carefully, and critically.

"If Jim doesn't kill me," she said to herself, "before

he takes a second look at me, he'll say I look like a Coney Island chorus girl. But what could I do—oh! what could I do with a dollar and eighty- seven cents?"

At 7 o'clock the coffee was made and the frying-pan was on the back of the stove hot and ready to cook the chops.

Jim was never late. Della doubled the fob chain in her hand and sat on the corner of the table near the door that he always entered. Then she heard his step on the stair away down on the first flight, and she turned white for just a moment. She had a habit for saying little silent prayers about the simplest everyday things, and now she whispered: "Please God, make him think I am still pretty."

The door opened and Jim stepped in and closed it. He looked thin and very serious. Poor fellow, he was only twenty-two—and to be burdened with a family! He needed a new overcoat and he was without gloves.

Jim stopped inside the door, as immovable as a set-ter at the scent of quail. His eyes were fixed upon Della, and there was an expression in them that she could not read, and it terrified her. It was not anger, nor surprise, nor disapproval, nor horror, nor any of the sen-timents that she had been prepared for. He simply stared at her fixedly with that peculiar expression on his face.

Della wriggled off the table and went for him.

"Jim, darling," she cried, "don't look at me that way. I had my hair cut off and sold because I couldn't have lived through Christmas without giving you a present. It'll grow out again—you won't mind, will you? I just had to do it. My hair grows awfully fast. Say 'Merry Christmas!' Jim, and let's be happy. You don't know what a nice—what a beautiful, nice gift I've got for you."

"You've cut off your hair?" asked Jim, laboriously, as if he had not arrived at that patent fact yet even after the hardest mental labor.

"Cut it off and sold it," said Della. "Don't you like me just as well, anyhow? I'm me without my hair, ain't I?"

Jim looked about the room curiously.

"You say your hair is gone?" he said, with an air almost of idiocy.

"You needn't look for it," said Della. "It's sold, I tell you—sold and gone, too. It's Christmas Eve, boy. Be good to me, for it went for you. Maybe the hairs of my head were numbered," she went on with sudden serious sweetness, "but nobody could ever count my love for you. Shall I put the chops on, Jim?"

Out of his trance Jim seemed quickly to wake. He enfolded his Della. For ten seconds let us regard with discreet scrutiny some inconsequential object in the other direction. Eight dollars a week or a million a year—what is the difference? A mathematician or a wit would give you the wrong answer. The magi brought valuable gifts, but that was not among them. This dark assertion will be illuminated later on.

Jim drew a package from his overcoat pocket and threw it upon the table.

"Don't make any mistake, Dell," he said, "about me. I don't think there's anything in the way of a hair-cut or a shave or a shampoo that could make me like my girl any less. But if you'll unwrap that package you may see why you had me going a while at first."

White fingers and nimble tore at the string and paper. And then an ecstatic scream of joy; and then, alas! a quick feminine change to hysterical tears and wails, necessitating the immediate employment of all the comforting powers of the lord of the flat.

For there lay The Combs —the set of combs, side and back, that Della had worshipped long in a Broadway window. Beautiful combs, pure tortoise shell, with jeweled rims—just the shade to wear in the beautiful vanished hair. They were expensive combs, she knew, and her heart had simply craved and yearned over them without the least hope of possession. And now, they were hers, but the tresses that should have adorned the coveted adornments were gone.

But she hugged them to her bosom, and at length she was able to look up with dim eyes and a smile and say: "My hair grows so fast, Jim!"

And them Della leaped up like a little singed cat and cried, "Oh, oh!"

Jim had not yet seen his beautiful present. She held it out to him eagerly upon her open palm. The dull precious metal seemed to flash with a reflection of her bright and ardent spirit.

"Isn't it a dandy, Jim? I hunted all over town to find it. You'll have to look at the time a hundred times a day now. Give me your watch. I want to see how it looks on it."

Instead of obeying, Jim tumbled down on the couch and put his hands under the back of his head and smiled.

"Dell," said he, "let's put our Christmas presents away and keep 'em a while. They're too nice to use just at present. I sold the watch to get the money to buy your combs. And now suppose you put the chops on."

The magi, as you know, were wise men—wonderfully wise men—who brought gifts to the Babe in the manger. They invented the art of giving Christmas presents. Being wise, their gifts were no doubt wise ones, possibly bearing the privilege of exchange in case of duplication. And here I have lamely related to you the uneventful chronicle of two foolish children in a flat who most unwisely sacrificed for each other the greatest treasures of their house. But in a last word to the wise of these days let it be said that of all who give gifts these two were the wisest. Of all who give and receive gifts, such as they are wisest. Everywhere they are wisest. They are the magi.

CHRISTMAS MORNING

"Christmas Morning at last!" every boy and girl said,
As without being told to, they jumped out of bed;
They'd being dreaming of Old Santa Clause, with a sack
Of presents and toys on his jolly broad back.
And the girls skipped for joy, and the boys gave a cheer,
"Hurrah!" they all cried, "Santa Claus has been here!"

It was true! Santa Claus had been—wasn't he kind?—
He'd left toys and presents for each one behind;
They wish'd they had beenawake when he came round,
To thank him for all the nice things that they found.

First a hamper for Dicky—what could be inside?
     "Oh make haste and open it," everyone cried;

Then a shout of excitement rang out on the air
    When 'twas found what good things in that big hamper
        were!
    Cakes and apples, and oh, Santa Claus must have
        guessed
    What each one just wanted and what all liked best.

Now, the day before Christmas young Dicky and Dolly
Had gone out together to gather some holly;
They worked very hard and brought back quite a stock,
Some they put on pictures, a piece on the clock!
    Wherever you looked there was some to be seen,
    With its pretty red berries and leaves of bright green;
    Although 'twas hard work, they all thought it fine fun,
    And the whole place looked beautiful when they had done.

For days in the kitchen had Cook with red face.
Been busy and bustling all over the place;

When they asked her "What is it?" she said "Wait and see!"
But without a plum pudding what would Christmas be?
That's what she was making—they guessed that from her—
And when it was finished they all had a stir;
Even Baby stirred too, with a serious look—
        "There, that's ready to go in the pot now," said Cook!

When breakfast was over they ran off in haste,
"Let's hurry," they cried, "not a moment we'll waste!"
Outside all the meadows were covered with snow.
        And soon a big snow man stood out there, you know,
        With umbrella, and kerchief, and hat on his head,
"Here's a fine Christmas snow man!" the boys and girls said.

To keep themselves warm next at snowballs they played.
The snow was so crisp,
   splendid snowballs
   it made:
They had a snow-battle,
   'twas capital fun,
Though nobody ever
   knew which side
   had won.
They made such a
   shouting, such
   noise and such
   clatter,
That Father came out
   to see what was the
   matter;

They pelted him finely with might and with main,
And made him fun back to his study again.

When the battle was
    done, they all went
    on the ice.
Where soon they
    found skating and
    sliding were nice;
Dolly sat on the
    bank, while Dick,
    the polite,
Put on her new
    skates for her,
    buckling them tight.

"Come on!" then he cried to the dear little maid,
"I'll take oh such care of you, don't be afraid!"
So she put her wee hands in his, "that's right," cried he,
And soon they were skating as well as could be.

But the best fun was when they tobogganing went,
What's a word by which, you must know,
sleighing is meant.

They sat on their sleighs and they slid down the hill,
　　　And now and then some of them had a fine spill.
It didn't much matter, so soft was the snow,
　　　To tumble would not hurt a baby, you know.

And as soon as they sleighed down,
　　　with might and with main
They dragged the sleigh up to the hill-top again.

If you'd heard how they laughed
　　　and had watched the fine fun,
You'd have said that of all sports, to sleigh was the one!

When tired of their sleighing, indoors they all ran,
To play "Hunt the Slipper," and "Catch me who can!"
They all of them sat in a ring on the ground.
And oh how they laughed when the slipper was found.
With crackers and many a Christmas Day game,
They passed the hours gaily till Dinner Time came!

The lamps were all lit, and the table was laid,
And oh what a dinner those little folks made:
Even Kitty for dinner a Christmas mouse had,
When she found it was clockwork it made her quite sad!

Then the pudding came in, all ablaze, you can see,
And all were as happy as happy could be:
When they thought of the fun they'd had, all gave a cheer,
And wished Christmas Day came round twelve
times a year!

HECTOR, THE DOG

Man loves the dog, the dog loves man:
　　The dog is trusty, strong, and brave,
And God has on the dog bestowed
　　The power and will man's life to save.

And often has the tale been told,
　　How, borne along in eager strife,
While struggling hard to rescue man,
　　The noble dog has lost his life.

*T*he little Inn of Martigny
　　Had but few guests on Christmas Eve,
For men at home made festive cheer,
　　And cared not household joys to leave.

But near the door the trav'ler stood,
　　Who with his host had earnest talk,
With knapsack girt and staff in hand,
　　All ready for a mountain walk.

"Nay, stay to-night; the way is long;
    Dark clouds are flitting o'er the sky;
A storm is brewing, trust my word,—
    I hear the raven's warning cry.

"Come, friend, give up thy toilsome walk,
And spend thy Christmas with us here."
The landlord spoke with kindly voice,
    Himself a well-trained mountaineer.

"Nay, press me not," the man replied;
    "I must get home by Christmas Day,
The mountain pass I know right well,
    Its hoary peaks and boulders gray.

Hector, the Dog

"Ten years ago I left my home
       My fortune in the world to seek;
It seems to me a long, long time
       Since last I saw these mountains bleak.

"I promised them that, come what might,
       I would be home on Christmas Day;
So farewell; may God's blessing be
       With me along my toilsome way."

In the fast-fading evening light
       He the pursued his lonely road,
Onward and upward through the snow,
       Leaving behind him man's abode.

Above him rose the snowy peaks,
       Still glowing white against the sky,
And many a crevasse, deep and wide,
       Around his path he could descry.

Upward and onward still he toil'd,
       His heart was beating loud and fast:
He'd reach'd his own dear fatherland—
       Danger and toil were well-nigh past.

He long'd to hear his father's voice,
       His mother's kiss once more to feel,
And in the quiet restful home
       With them once more in prayer to kneel.

He long'd to spread before their gaze
       The honest gains of many a year,
Earn'd with hard toil for those he lov'd
       And guarded with a jealous care.

His father, with his silver hair;
    His mother, with her kind blue eyes:
His sisters, little playmates once—
    Would he their faces recognize?

Colder and colder blew the wind,
    It whistled up the mountain-pass,
The blinding snow-storm flew before;
    The ice was slippery as glass.

Onward he went, but cautiously;
    "Surely I have not miss'd my way?
The night grows dark, 'tis piercing cold:
    Can I hold on till dawn of day?"

And still he battled with the storm,
    That every moment fiercer grew,
And stronger came the dreadful thought
    That he the way no longer knew.

And now his strength is ebbing fast;
    His head is sinking on his breast.
Oh! could he in that fearful storm
    But find some shelter, gain some rest!

Happy for him that at that time,
    Alone upon the mountain-side,
He knew that to his Father's love,
    His life or death he might confide.

The eddying snow-wreath whirl'd around,
    Snow hid the path, snow fill'd the air.
He fell unconscious to the ground,
    The object of a Father's care.

Above the smooth white-sheeted snow
    The convent-walls rose dark and high,
And bright the clear, cold stars look'd down
    From out the wind-swept winter sky.

The stately shadows, broad and dark,
    Lay stretch'd along the mountain-side,
And through the narrow windows gleam'd
    The blazing logs of Christmas-tide.

It was the hold Christmas Eve,
    When joy in Christian homes should be:
And in this lonely monast'ry
    Was friendly talk and quiet glee.

And truly none deserved it more
    Than these lone men of lowly mind,
Who, in their Master's steps to tread.
    Had left the pleasant world behind.

That was a scene for painter's art,
    Those men so calm, so free from strife,
Who bore upon each rugged fact
    The impress of a noble life.

Nor men alone composed the group:
    Four dogs, of pure St. Bernard blood,
Or slept unconscious on the hearth,
    Or by their masters proudly stood;

Hector, the Dog

Calm, lofty, steadfast, great and strong,
    A picture of the mountains round;
Both dogs and masters in one tie
    Of kindly brotherhood fast bound.

What was their life? Had selfish aim
    Enticed them to this lonely spot;
Life's toil and burden to escape,
    It's battle-field to enter not.

No, surely: not in sinful ease
    The daily life of each was spent,
But to fight hand in hand with Death
    Each nerve was strain'd, each power bent.

For here, amongst the snow and ice,
    The everlasting winter cold,
Full many a weary traveler
    Had died unknown since days of old.

And so to seek and save the lost
    These men and dogs were living here;
Bravely they daily risked their,
    Nor e'er gave way to thought of fear.

Vespers are over. In the hall
    The monks are gather'd round the board
To celebrate the joyful feast
    With the best cheer their stores afford.

The noble dogs are feasting now,
    Fed with kind hands and loving care:
For if they share their masters' toils
    Their joys and feasts they also share

"Brethren and friends," the Prior said,
    "The night grows wild, the storm gets high,
The dogs are restless; some must go,
    If help is needed, to be nigh.

"This night we'll sing our hymn to God
    With shepherds and the angelic host;
But you will praise whilst yet you serve
    And by the serving praise Him most."

So, taking hatchets, torches, ropes,
    The monks and dogs together went;
They make towards the mountain pass,
    And soon the dogs are on a scent.

Smelling and sniffing through the storm,
    Their noble heads bent to the snow,
Close follow'd by the stalwart monks,
    They bravely up the mountain go.

"Full sure, I guess," said Brother Ralph,
    "Some traveler is out to-night,
And sure I am that for his life
    With storm and snow he'll have to fight.

"And if but once he miss the path,
    Hard by the precipice which winds,
A fearful sight 'twill be for him
    The mangled traveler that finds.

"But, see, the dogs are on the track;
    See how with one consent they go;
They've turn'd the point, they're out of sight:
    And, hark! That baying down below!"

The monks rush on with breathless speed,
   All on the strain, no word they say;
But as they breast the storm-blasts' rage,
   With silent earnestness they pray.

They turn the point, and down below
   The eager, striving dogs they see,
All on a narrow ledge that hangs
   Projecting o'er the icy sea.

There's once way down, but e'en in light,
   When all is calm, on summer's day,
While in pursuit of mountain goat,
   The hunter dreads that dizzy way.

The brothers pause, and peering down,
   Each grasps the other as he stands;
The noble hounds will do till death
   What their life-saving law commands.

First one and then the other down
   That fearful steep, with shuddering cry,
They creep, they cringe, they bound, they roll,
   And now on snow-slip swiftly fly.

The snow-slip takes a happy turn,
   And lands them on the icy sea,
And sharp glad barkings upward send
   The tidings of their victory.

And thanks to God! The storm is past
   The gentle moon gives out her light
To guide their footsteps down each steep,
   And aid their swing from height to height.

Hector, the Dog

They reach at length the sea of ice,
    Three dogs came bounding to their side:
They fourth, brave Hector, where was he
    Hurl'd by the avalanche's slide?

Anxious and eager rush the dogs
    To where a face of hopeful glow
And firm resolve, in death-like swoon,
    Peers upward from the open'd snow.

What dogs could do these dogs have done;
    Man's skill and care must do the rest;
And sooner far than could be thought
    Their efforts with success were blest.

But other cares await them now
    No sooner had they shown the man,
Then, darting off with eager haste,
    The hounds to farther distance ran.

Hector they seek, with whine and cries;
    They scratch the appalling mound of snow,
Which, loosen'd from the mountainside,
    Had swept them with it down below.

Vain work for dogs! Vain work for men!
    Thousands of tons of ice and snow,
Heap'd up in one vast funeral pile
    Poor Hector hold entombed below.

Alas! Poor Hector! Gone for him
    Those scampers on the mountain side,
Where to lead men from height to height
    Still upward, was his joy and pride.

Gone the sweet smell of pine-clad hill,
　　The bright blue sky, the sunny slope,
The torrent's roar, the eagle's cry,
　　The foes with which he used to cope.

For winter oft would send the wolf
　　To prowl among the flocks below,
And oft the bear would seek the herds
　　That shudder'd on their path of snow.

Then mighty courage filled the heart
Of Hector, bravest of the brave!
And forth he rushed, with eager haste,
　　The trembling flocks and herds to save.

But now no more! his work is done;
　　The dog has met a hero's end!
With deep drawn sigh the brethren mourn
　　Their mute companion and their friend.

Then on, with heavy hearts, and slow,
　　They bear with toil the rescued man,
Mounting still upward to the height
　　From whence their steep descent began.

And slow, and hanging low their heads,
　　As if oppress'd by sense of shame
Mingled with grief, the noble hounds
　　In silence to the convent came.

There watchful care attends the couch
　　Where rests the traveler return'd,
And swift feet carry to his home
　　Good news of one they might have mourn'd.

But as each Christmas-tide return'd,
    And still he toil'd in life's rough way
With thankful praise he join'd in thought
    Hector, the dog, and Christmas Day.

"Unless we make Christmas and occasion to share our blessings, all the snow in Alaska won't make it 'white'."

—Bing Crosby

HOW TO MAKE
SNOW HOUSES, SNOW MEN,
AND SNOW ANIMALS

*T*HE Eskimo uses a bone-bladed knife to cut the snow into the blocks with which he builds his winter home; but our snow is seldom, if ever, hard and compact enough to admit of this treatment and we must find another way to handle it.

When the snow is damp, start with a small snowball and roll it until it has increased to the size you wish. During the process of rolling the ball, it must be frequently turned on its base, so that it will be round and solid and not a loose, oblong cylinder like a roll of cotton batting.

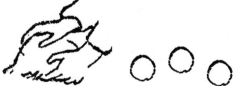

Make a number of these snowballs and pile them up into a heap the form of a haystack; pound and hammer the balls together, filling up all the cracks and crevices with broken pieces packed tightly in place.

AFTER THE SNOWBALLS HAVE BEEN WELDED

together into a compact mass of snow, take shovels and scrapers made of thin boards or shingles and scrape the surface of your snow mound until it is smooth, symmetrical and of the form of half an egg.

NEXT, CUT A NUMBER OF STICKS;

make them each exactly 2 feet in length and, after pointing one end of every stick, drive them all into the snow mound until their heads are even of flush with the surface of the snow. The sticks should be distributed over the mound at regular intervals so that the pointed inside ends may guide you while hollowing out the interior of your house and prevent you from making the walls of unequal thickness. You can now cut a doorway just big enough to allow you to creep in on all fours.

WHEN EXCAVATING THE INSIDE

watch for the pointed ends of the measuring pegs, and do not dig beyond them; the walls of the igloo must be at least 2 feet thick to prevent the structure from crumbling down upon the heads of the Eskimos (?) inside, and also that it may withstand any ordinary thaw without disintegrating. If

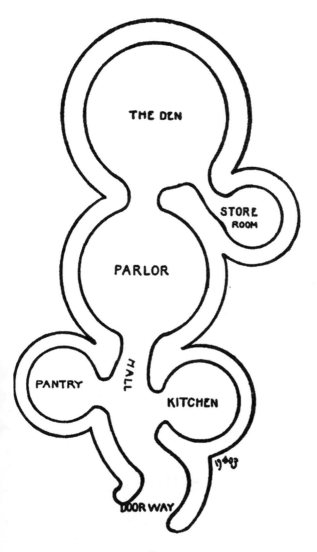

FIG. 1
THE GROUND PLAN
OF AN IGLOO

THE SITE CHOSEN FOR THE IGLOO

be in a shady place the snow house will last longer than when exposed to the direct rays of the winter's sun, but even in the sun a well-made snow house of this description will ofttimes remain intact long after the surrounding snow has disappeared.

AFTER BUILDING AN IGLOO,

as described above, if you are still ambitious to do more in this line, Fig. 1 shows the ground plan for a commodious Eskimo apartment house, and Fig. 2 shows a diagram of the outside of this compound igloo.

Although the illustration shows this snow house with the division lines as if build of snow blocks, it is

FIG. 2
RECONSTRUCTION OF AN IGLOO
FIRST OCCUPIED BY DOCTOR HALL,
THE ARCTIC EXPLORER

nevertheless to be built of solid snow and hollowed out as already described, but to make it appear like the real thing, the snow blocks can be imitated by lines drawn with the pointed end of a measuring peg. The window is made of a piece of ice set in the snow at the opening cut for that purpose.

To build this house, make the "den" or big igloo, first, as already described; from the waste snow build the little igloo marked "storeroom," then add the one marked "parlor" and from the waste snow of the last build the pantry. Next add the kitchen and the low entrance. When this is accomplished you will have a duplicate of the first igloo occupied by that daring Arctic explorer, Doctor Hall.

The Doctor slept on a snow shelf in the part we call the "den," cooked over a whale-oil lamp in the room marked kitchen, and kept his frozen provisions in the storeroom, where they were safe from the wolfish dogs.

The great advantage of all these passages and rooms in a boy's snow house is the feasibility of sealing the doorway of the storeroom or even the den itself with snow, so that a stranger entering the house will never suspect the presence of these extra rooms, but will creep out again under the impression that he has explored the whole interior.

Neither will he discover his mistake unless he makes inside and outside measurements, and by this means finds a large, unaccounted-for space; but vagrant boys do not use this much care, and are never scientific in their investigations. So the contents of the den and storeroom will be comparatively safe.

SNOW MEN AND ANIMALS

Since snow is easily carved and modeled, there is no good reason why statues of some merit should not replace the grotesque effigies which most men have build during the days of their boyhood. The better the work the more enjoyable the occupation, the more fun there is in the doing of it.

In place of building a figure by sticking lumps of snow on to other lumps, balls for eyes and ears and another ball for a nose, why not make a solid block of snow and carve the face from it?

Suppose A (Fig. 1) to be a snow block, B then shows the first effects of carving, C the next step, and in D we already have the semblance of a head and bust; E begins to show some likeness to a well-known American, and F and G, Fig. 2 may be passed upon an unsuspecting public as a portrait of the Father of Our Country.

In making this bust, remember and make the epaulets limp, mere bands of braid with fringe on edge, for that is the kind worn at that date—the upholstered epaulets seen upon the statues in New York City and

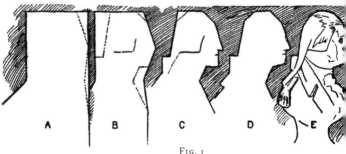

FIG. 1
THE EVOLUTION OF THE PROFILE

FIG. 2
THE FINISHED BUST
G. PROFILE VIEW
F. FRONT VIEW

elsewhere were not invented until after Washington's death, and like the sword of 1861, which the bronze Washington usually carries, are simply marks of the sculptor's ignorance or carelessness.

If you make a snow man,

MAKE HIM RIGHT!

Of course there are many to whom these diagrams (A to G) will be of little assistance, but even untrained eyes and unskilled hands can do a thing mechanically, for that requires only care and patience. So, though you may not be able to make anything more resembling Washington than the background figure with a hat in Fig. 2, you may at least make a statue of the beast Washington drove from this country. (Fig. 3).

Build a solid snow block 7 squares long by 8 squares high and 4 squares broad. These squares may be of any size you find convenient, 6 inches or 1 foot, or greater or less. See the small diagram at bottom of Fig. 4. This block of snow should rest upon a rough base to elevate it above the ground. With a board and rule or string and wooden pegs divide the snow block as shown by Figs. 4 and 5. Take this book in the left hand, a pointed stick in the right hand and sketch the outline of the lion.

Placing the point of the stick a trifle to the left of the middle of the square (1,2) and tracing a line through 1 to a point a quarter of the distance from 1 to 0 and half way between the line A and 1, thence perpendicularly down, crossing the line A and swinging off diagonally to a point in the line 0 a quarter distant between B and C, thence to a point on C a quarter distant from line 1, thence down diagonally to a point just to the right of 1 and above D, and so on as shown in the diagram.

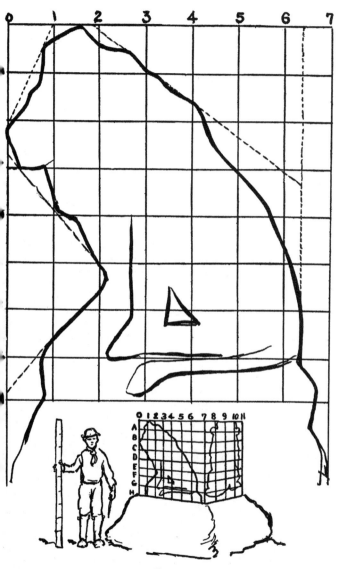

FIG. 4
BLOCKED AND SKETCHED
READY TO BE CARVED

FIG. 5
REAR AND FRONT VIEWS
OF THE SNOW LION

When this is done the artist will find that he has traced out a duplicate of the diagram (Fig. 4). If he will now trace the heavy outlines of the front and rear view shown by Fig. 5, he will have something to guide him in cutting away the snow. The dotted lines show the first cuts to make on the profile view; but it will possibly be wise for him to leave the front until the last so that the outlines of front view will be there to guide him. These he may cut away on one side back to the front legs, before he finishes the profile.

A few experiments will teach him how the thing is done, and if he makes a mistake it may be rectified by plastering the snow back firmly in place and trying it again.

There is a chunk of snow left between the legs to give stability to the statue, and the legs are carved in high relief, but the snow is left under the body for support. The texture of hair on the mane and head may be reproduced by using a coarse comb.

The squares on the lion may have sides of 6 inches, 12 inches, or any dimensions the would-be sculptor may choose so long as all sides are equal.

If these directions are followed, with a copy of this book in your hand for reference, the result will no doubt be a surprise to your friends and a proportional subject of pride to yourself.

After acquiring some skill, the beginner can take any picture of a man or woman, divide it into squares, and reproduce a creditable copy in snow.

A grotesque portrait can be modeled by marking the divisions, as described, on the picture to be copied, but making them of unequal sides on the snow block; for instance, if the sides are 16 inches broad and 10 inches high you will elongate your subject to a ridiculous degree, and if the copy is made with divisions of 6 inches high and 10 inches wide, you will broaden the figure to a laughable extent. In any case you will pass a few hours in a healthy outdoor pursuit, and come indoors with red cheeks and an appetite which demands immediate attention.

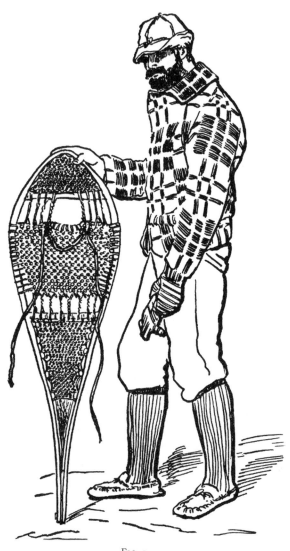

FIG. 1
SKETCH OF A MAIN WOODMAN AND HIS SNOW-SHOE

SNOW SHOES, HOW TO MAKE 'EM, PUT THEM ON AND WALK IN THEM

A REVIEW of the snow fields will reveal all sorts of appliances for binding the snow-shoes to the feet, and every expert and experienced snow-shoer, apparently, has an individual fastening of his own upon which he places the greatest reliance.

Some shoes have leather slipper toes attached to them, others broad leather straps and buckles, some simply toe straps (see Fig. 4) and thongs, and others naught but the buckskin thong, the same as the American Indians were using long before Columbus came blundering around their coast in search of East India.

To prevent a confusing of terms in speaking of the parts of the snow-shoe, let us adopt nautical names. By reference to Fig. 1 it will be seen that the snow-shoe is shaped like an elongated bow kite; this is the most familiar form, and, although some shoes vary greatly from the one shown in the illustration, they all agree in their general anatomy with this diagram.

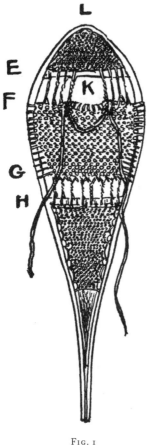

FIG. I
SNOW-SHOE

By applying nautical terms the toe (L) becomes the bow, the heel (J) the stern, and the cross stocks E and H are the thwarts. F and G are simply thongs to which the coarser net-work between them is attached. K is the hole for the toe of the moccasin. At the two lower corners of the toe hole will be found eyelets made of strengthened meshes. The framework is usually made of second growth white-ash wood, the meshes are of rawhide; from L to E and H to J the net-work is finely woven, but from F to G, amidship, it must bear the weight of the man, the net is here made of heavier material and with much coarser meshes. It will be seen by further reference to the illustration that a thong is so strung through the eyelets that the long ends come up between the wide meshes each side of the toe hole (K, Fig. 1), thus forming a loop or toe-strap into which the toe of your moccasined foot is to be thrust; by drawing the ends of the thongs, the loop may be pulled down to fit snugly across the toe of the moccasin (A, Fig. 2). If your thongs be short an economical tie will be the one shown by B (Fig. 2); to make this, pass one end of the thong under the toe loop, up and back over the same loop, then under itself, making a half hitch on the toe loop; from here it is brought back behind the moccasin, where it meets the other end of the thong, which has been half hitched to the opposite side of the toe loop, as in B (Fig. 2). At the heel of the moccasin the ends pass under and over each other as shown in the diagram, then come around the ankle and tie in a square knot in front. This, as may be seen, leaves the heel free to move up and down in a natural manner (a, Fig.2).

The freedom of the heel is necessary, and the toe hole (K, Fig. 1) permits a free movement of the toes, the foot being fastened only at the toe joints to the cross thong F (Fig. 1). It must be remembered that in

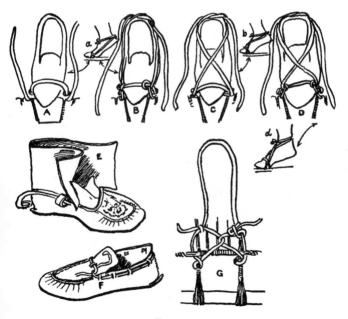

Fig. 2
Two Moccassins and Some Ways Snow-shoes Are Fastened

using snow-shoes the latter are lifted no higher than is necessary to clear the surface of the snow; in fact, a man walking with snow-shoes scuffs along much the same as a man with slipshod slippers run down at the heels. Another way to tie on the snow-shoe is to simply pull the slack of the toe loop down to fit over the toe of the moccasin by drawing the ends of the thongs, as in Fig. 6, then crossing them over the instep and bringing them back over the heel of the moccasin as shown by diagram C (Fig. 2), and fastening the ends around the ankle (b, Fig. 2). But the manifest objection to this method is that there is nothing but the friction of the moccasin to prevent the thong from slipping and sawing; this, however, can be remedied by a half hitch at each side of the toe, as is done at B (Fig. 2), and is shown with the cross bands over the instep by D and d, Fig. 2).

E and F (Fig. 2) show two styles of moccasins most frequently seen on snow-shoes in the northern United States, New Brunswick and Southern Canada, and G the one string hitch.

It is probably with good reason that the majority of men whom necessity compels to use snow-shoes, prefer a tie which brings one or more strands of the thong alongside of the foot, as shown by a and B (Fig. 2), and it is also evident that the cross bands over the instep give greater security to the fastening. So a method which combines the instep cross bands and the heel bands has much to recommend it. Fig. 3, G H I J, shows the evolution of such a tie with a double toe loop. The heel loop, however, is made first as shown by Fig. 5, then the double toe loop is made by passing each end of the thong through the opposite eyelet hole, as shown by G (Fig. 3). Next a half hitch is taken over the double toe loop exactly as was done

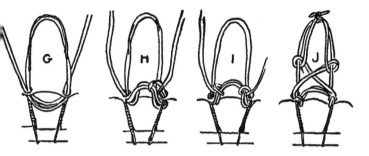

FIG. 3
ANOTHER GOOD HITCH

with the single loop (B and D, Fig. 2) and is now shown by H and I (Fig. 3). After which the ends are crossed over the instep, half hitched on each side over the heel loop and brought back behind the foot (J, Fig. 3), where the two ends are tied in a reefing or square knot. Much of the intricateness of this last hitch may be obviated by the use of the tussle-logan toe strap, which is a permanent affair woven in through the meshes down each side astern of the eyelet holes (Fig. 4). Put the two ends of your thong down through the eyelet holes and bring them up between the wide meshes astern of the bow thwart, as shown by Fig. 5. Slip the toe of your moccasin under the tussle-logan, and, by drawing on the ends of the thong, pull the band snugly around your heel (Fig. 6). Next take a half hitch (O and N, Fig. 7) around the

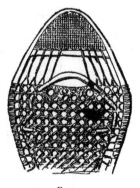

FIG. 4
THE TUSSLE-LOGAN
TOE STRAP

FIG. 5
PUTTING ON THE
SNOW-SHOE

FIG. 6
PULL BAND SNUGGLY
AROUND THE HEEL

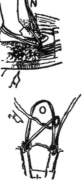

FIG. 7
HOW THE HALF-HITCH
IS MADE AND THE SIDE
OF THE FOOT

x

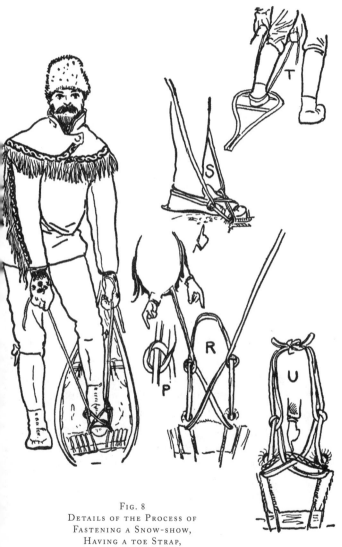

FIG. 8
DETAILS OF THE PROCESS OF
FASTENING A SNOW-SHOW,
HAVING A TOE STRAP,
TO THE FOOT

FIG. 9
READY TO TIE THONGS BACK
OF THE HEELS

side band and draw it taut, as in the illustration. Go through the same process as shown by P R S (Fig. 8), and draw tight, as the man is doing in the same illustration. T is a back view of this process. When the tussle-logan happens to fit the toe too loosely, it may be made secure by passing the cross straps in and over, as shown at U (Fig. 8). Fig. 9 shows a snow-shoer bringing the free ends of the thong back behind the heel, preparatory to fastening them there with a tie. V shows the thong properly fastened (the tussle-logan omitted for the sake of simplicity in the diagram). W shows the knot as tied in the Maine woods. Fig. 10 shows a man with snow-shoes on both feet, and X, Y and Z are from sketches of snow-shoers in motion, made in Michigan, Canada and the Maine woods.

FIG. 10
THE SNOW-SHOE IN USE

A Tussle-Logan Toe Strap

on a shoe possesses many advantages for one who must needs use snow-shoes every time necessity compels travel during the winter months, and not the least of these advantages is the fact that after one's shoes have once been satisfactorily adjusted they need not be untied again until the thongs break or some similar accident renders a readjustment necessary.

The lad in Fig. 11 has one shoe on, and is in the act of slipping his foot into the thongs of the second shoe. It will be seen that he takes a pose like an old-fashioned dancing master, with his toes turned out; this is done so that he can slip his toes over the first side of the heel loop and under the second side, as is better explained by the empty moccasin (a, Fig. 11). Next he thrusts his foot so far that the heel comes under the

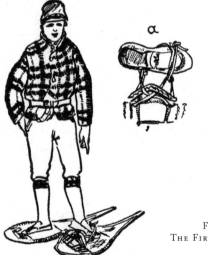

FIG. 11
THE FIRST POSITION

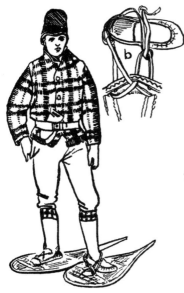

FIG. 12
THE SECOND POSITION

FIG. 13
THE THIRD POSITION

heel loop (b, Fig. 12). Then, lifting his heel and pointing his toes down (d, Fig. 13) he so twists his foot that the toe of his moccasin slips under the tussle-logan and the shoe is adjusted and ready to support him on drifts and fields of snow.

Three figures and three diagrams have been made of this act so that the reader may not fail to understand how it is done, but because so many pictures are necessary to make the explanation clear it must not be supposed that this manner of putting on a snow-shoe is either difficult or intricate; it is accomplished in much less time than it requires to tell how it is done, and is really only one continuous movement of the foot like one step in dancing.

Now that you know how to put on snow-shoes, take them down from the wall where you hung them as a decoration for the library, dining-room or den and sally forth, but do not put them on in the house as did the writer in his first attempt to master the art. There is no enacted law to prevent you from adjusting the shoes indoors, but it is better to do it outside, where there is more room and not steps to descend.

The writer forgot about the steps; his only idea was to sneak out the back way unobserved, but he did not succeed, and in going down the steps the long heels of the snow-shoes made it necessary to step sideways. After the first step it was impossible for him to take another; he could not lift his foot more than an inch, and in spite of a struggle which nearly wrenched the thongs from the feet he stood as securely fastened to the step as if his shoes were nailed down, and it really seemed that they had frozen to the snow. The long heel of the one bearing his weight lay across the heel of the one he was struggling to lift. In regard to a

PROPER SNOW-SHOE COSTUME

it will probably be found that the mackinaw blanket coat worn by all lumbermen is best adapted to this purpose. The lumbermen also wear thick woolen stockings outside of their trousers and call them leggings. These are very comfortable, but they give the leg a thick, bulky appearance, which can be avoided by wearing knickerbockers and long stockings. Short woolen socks can be worn with advantage over the long ones, and tightly rolled down to the top of the moccasin, which will keep out the snow.

The mackinaw coats can be purchased at any outfitting establishment. Some of these blanket coats are very beautiful and some as gaudy as an Indian chief in war paint. One suit in my costume chest consists of a blue and yellow striped coat and scarlet trousers with a blue plaid, the squares of which are about 6 inches broad. This loud dress I bought at a lumber camp in northern Michigan. Formerly, lumbermen, Indians and snow-shoers wore a red silk of worsted scarf about their middle, but now it is seldom seen, a strap, or the belt of the jacket itself answering the purpose.

There is but one positive rule for the snow-shoer concerning his dress and that is he must wear moccasins, but the rest of his clothes may be anything that his taste and comfort direct.

The mackinaw coat is shown in several of the diagrams, and Fig. 1 (on page 224) shows the complete winter costume of a lumberman.

Fig. 1   Fig. 2
TOOLS USED AND PARTS NECESSARY
IN THE CONSTRUCTION OF A JUMPER

HOW TO MAKE FOUR SIMPLE (AND NOT SO SIMPLE) SLED DESIGNS

1.
How to Build a Jumper, or Humpdurgin, and a Gummer in the Woods

*T*HE only really necessary tools with which to work in building a jumper is an axe and an auger, but for that reason one need not throw away the contents of the tool chest.

The jumper is a sleigh made from green wood, cut in the forest for the occasion; hickory saplings furnish the proper material and the denser the forest the taller and straighter the saplings will be. These are the sort of sticks you should seek for

THE RUNNERS

of the proposed sleigh (Fig. 1). With a good sharp axe, lop off the branches, leaving no projecting stubs; then cut two more stout sticks like the one marked with large capitals A B C D E (Fig. 2) for the top rails of the runners; after which lay the top rail on a level piece of ground and the long bottom rail alongside of it at exactly the distance from the top rail which you have decided to be the height of the proposed runner (Fig. 2). Next cut the spokes AF, BG, CH, DJ and EK, and lay them along the runners, in the positions which you intend them to occupy in the finished frame (Fig. 2), and mark where they are to be trimmed down to fit the proposed auger holes in rail, at A B C D E, and runner at F G H J K. also mark the places for the auger holes and scratch the direction, or angle, on the rail and runner of the slanting auger holes at the ends of the sleigh AF and EK (Fig. 2). This done, bore the auger holes at the points marked, being careful to make the middle ones at right angles with the rail and runner, and the end ones to exactly correspond with the diagonal scratches made to guide you. Now test your spokes and see that the middle ones are of equal length and end ones of proper length to fit holes EK, AF. Trim off the spokes so that they may be forced into the holes and then drive them in place.

Take care not to make the ends of the spokes so large as to split your rail or runner or to drive them in with such force as to produce the same disastrous result; they need to be firmly fixed in place, but not forced into the auger holes with sledge hammer blows.

THE SHAFTS

of this jumper are the long protruding ends of the runners, and if the wood proves to be too stiff to bend properly for the correct angle of the shafts, the top of the runners may be carefully shaved off at the bending point in front of the sleigh as it is in Fig. 2. But do not do this until you have completed your jumper and tested the elasticity of the poles by lifting up the ends of the shafts, something after the manner the Yale man is doing in Fig. 3.

When one runner is finished to your satisfaction build a duplicate one as already described.

THE AUGER HOLES

may go entirely through the top rail, but must not go through the runners, for the obvious reason that if the spokes protrude through the runners they will retard the progress of the sleigh. For ordinary purposes it is not necessary to have as many spokes to runners as are shown in Figs. 2 and 3, but the builder must here use his own judgment, as he must also do in the selection of the material. Green white ash can be split with a nail.

It requires more skill to build a light jumper than a heavy one, and the best course for a novice to pursue is to select timber heavy enough to avoid any great danger of splitting it when the spokes are driven in place.

THE FRAME

of the sleigh is finished when the cross braces are put in place (Fig. 3) and secured there by nails, withes or lashings of thongs, twine or marline (Fig. 4). A glance at Fig. 3 will show the reader that, within reasonable limits, the greater

FIG. 3 NOTICE THAT THE SHAFTS ARE CUT THINNER NEAR FRONT OF RUNNERS SO HAT THEY MAY BEND AT THESE POINTS

the weight which rests on the runners, the less liability there is of the spokes working out of their bearings.

THE BRACES

may have log cabin joints to fit in similar ones cut in the top fail as shown by small diagrams marked "joints" (Fig. 3) or, if there is thought to be any danger of weakening the top rails by these joints, or if the builder is in haste, the braces can be nailed in place without having any notches at all.

THE GUMMER

is a hand sled built on the general plans of the jumper, and it is called a gummer because it is somewhat similar to the ones used by the men known as gummers who live in the forests and make their living by collecting spruce gum for children and "sales-ladies" to chew.

FIG. 4 THE CONSTRUCTION AND USE OF THE GUMMER

THE RUNNERS OF A GUMMER

are lower in proportion to its size than are those of a jumper, but they are made in the same manner as the latter. The reader will of course understand that a gummer is built of very much lighter material than a jumper.

As may be seen by reference to Fig. 4 the runners are bent up until they reach the protruding ends of the top rails, when they are securely bound in place with thongs, or fastened by nails to a cross-piece which is omitted in the illustration.

If you are the happy possessor of a piece of board

The Top of the Gummer

may be made of this, but to many minds the presence of a piece of sawed lumber savors too strongly of the effete civilization of towns and cities. In the woods one likes to have

The Real Thing

which, in this case, is a top made of halved pieces of spruce, pine or other wood, or of shakes, splits or clapboards, as the small, rough boards split by woodmen from quartered logs are variously called, according to the locality in which one happens to be camping. Fig. 5 shows a low sledge built jumper style, but with an elevated seat and

Fig. 5 In the woods one likes to have the real thing

A Tandem Rig

This is used in narrow trails which exist in some sections where roads are wanting and where the winter snows smooth the trails by obliterating the stones and logs which impede summer travel.

The Body of a Jumper

can be finished in any style which one's time and material will allow. A good top for a jumper can be made in the same manner as the runners; that is, by the use of spokes and a rail, as is shown in Fig. 6. Straw or hay may be used for seats, if there is any such material obtainable, and if not, one can fill the crib with the sweet smelling balsam, upon which we all love to sleep while in the woods. The balsam may not be so warm as hay or straw, but it is soft to sit upon, while its perfume appeals to one's poetic idea of the forest; and blankets and wraps may be depended upon to keep out the frosts, as one goes bouncing over the "thank you marms" in the improvised sleigh, proud to be a real exemplification of

The Simple Life

It will be noticed that the jumper in Fig. 6 has the top rail of the runner prolonged into shafts and the lower rails of the runner curved up and made fast to the shafts. This can sometimes be done when the sleigh is so light that the stiffness of the runners, if prolonged into shafts, would cause the jumper to rear up on its hind legs, so to speak. Yet the wood may be elastic enough to be forced up to the upper rail of the runner and made fast there, as it is in Fig. 6.

When you have horses, you, in all probability, also have wagons, and in that case it may be possible to take

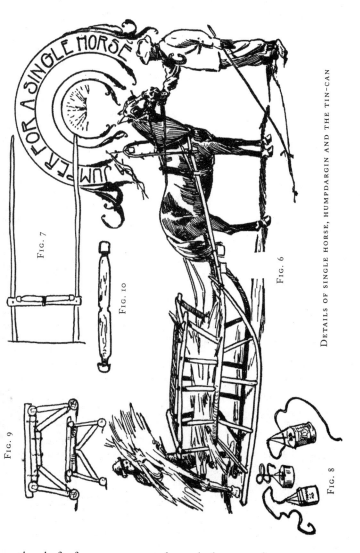

FIG. 7

FIG. 10

FIG. 6

FIG. 9

FIG. 8

DETAILS OF SINGLE HORSE, HUMPDARGIN AND THE TIN-CAN

the shafts from a wagon and attach them to a jumper, or
it may save time and labor to remove the whiffletree
from one of the wheeled conveyances and attach it to
the sleigh, to which to fasten the traces.

But if there are no wagons handy there will probably be no traces, and in that case ropes must supply the
place of traces and reins. With ropes for traces a rude

Whiffletree

may be made of a stick notched at the end to receive
the rope and notched in the middle, where it is bound
to the cross-brace between the shafts, as shown by Figs.
7 and 10. In the illustrations good harness is depicted
upon the horses, but that is because they are picture-
horses, and good harness is always as acceptable to the
illustrator as is bad, or improvised, and looks much better than either; but in the woods, with only packhorses
at one's command, improvised harness of ropes or
thongs will probably be the only kind available, and a
breast strap must then be substituted for the collars
worn by the animals in the diagrams.

Home Made Sleigh Bells

are not a difficult proposition to one who wishes them
for use and not appearances, and tobacco, meat, or
tomato cans, which are to be found around almost any
camp, will be as much admired by the deer, moose,
wolves, coons or jack rabbits as the most expensive
Russian sleigh bells. If a few round pebbles be placed
inside of the cans they will make as much noise as necessary to apprise any other wayfarer of the approach of
the jumper. Fig. 8 shows how the cans may be hung by
strings run through nail holes, and Fig. 6 shows some
such crude bells attached to the shafts of the jumper.

It is possible that one may want to build a heavy
sledge on the jumper plan, for the "toting" of weighty
dunnage or heavy material of some sort, and in that case
the ordinary jumper runners, if made tall, even when

built of heavy material, may be liable to spread, or fold up under the sleigh. Fig. 9 shows a cross-section of a jumper with braces to prevent such accidents, simple affairs nailed in place so as to stiffen the frame. As emergencies arise change the shape to suit the conditions, while keeping the real essentials.

2.
How to Make a Skiboggan, a Barrel-stave Toboggan, and a Togoggan-bob

*I*n the New England States, where the snow is seldom soft and often is coated with a hard crust of ice, the runners of the native sleds, only a few inches in height, appear very low compared with the Ohio sled; even sleds with no runners at all are sometimes used. On steep, icy hills any old thing will slide, and here it is that the

SKIBOGGAN

is seen in all its glory. In construction this cranky sled is simplicity itself, but its successful use requires an expert, and there will be many a tumble for the beginner in the art of skibogganing.

If you live in the country, go to the woodpile and find a round cord-wood stick no wider than the stout barrel stave selected for your runner. Saw the cord-wood stick so that it will stand perpendicularly when it is fastened to the stave at a third of the distance from one end (Fig. 11). If cord-wood is not available, take a piece of studding 4 x 4 or 2 x 4 and use that. With the convex side of the stave underneath, lay it over the block and nail it securely in place; reverse it, and you

FIG. 11

FIG. 12

A STAVE SKIBOGGAN

have Fig. 11. The comfort of the rider demands a seat, which can be made of a small piece of thin board fastened T-wise on the block (Fig. 12).

With the long end of the stave in front of you, seat yourself on the T saddle with your feet on the snow on each side of the runner and start down hill. The skiboggan can be used on hills which are so steep as to make the use of an ordinary sled impracticable.

The best skiboggans are made of the staves of sugar hogs-heads or oil-barrel staves, and the upright post is braced upon each side by parts of barrel staves thus)|(, or with bits of plank thus /|\. But if you are going to put much work on the thing, you might as well build a really good

BARREL-STAVE TOBOGGAN

Winter weather frequently brings a good deal of dry, soft snow which won't pack and makes ordinary sledding laborious. The narrow runners sink through quickly, and the average boy finds himself longing for a toboggan of some sort. If he has no toboggan, however, it is a simple matter to nail some pieces across two or three barrel staves and thus secure a rude but very serviceable substitute.

The serious defect of a barrel-stave toboggan like

this is that it has not the high-rolling front of the real American toboggan, and consequently is liable to bury itself in the first hummock of snow encountered by the coaster, or to stick its nose in the snow, "turn turtle" and throw over the boy who is using it. It was these little eccentricities of the stave sled which led the writer to produce the toboggans shown in the accompanying illustrations and diagrams, and reference to them will show you how the faults may be overcome by the insertion of bow and stern pieces cut from strips of plank nailed together or of blocks of wood sawed from the end of a 4 x 4 inch post. Such a toboggan can be used alone (Fig. 23) or joined to another (as in Figs. 32, 33 and 34) by a reach-board and thus form a unique machine which we shall call the toboggan-bob.

Any boy who can manage a saw and drive a nail can make one of the toboggans, and any boy with skill in carpentry can build a good bob from the material usually to be found in the back yard, cellar, or attic.

No Really Good Results

can be obtained by the use of poor lumber, but if good lumber proves too costly, excellent oil-barrels can be purchased from dealers. Casks such as are used to catch rain-water have smooth, stiff staves and are well adapted for the purpose of the sledge-builder. Again, you can buy a very good sugar-barrel at your grocer's for 15 cents, and although the wood is not so good or the staves so well made as those in an oil-barrel, still there are some of them good enough to make very serviceable bottom pieces for the runners, and the rougher staves can be used for the top parts.

As has already been suggested, the advantage of a barrel-stave toboggan-bob over the ordinary double-runner sled-bob is three-fold: the former may be used

on snow which is too soft for the narrow runners of the
common sled, the materials for its construction are more
easily obtained, and it requires less skill to build.

THE MATERIALS NECESSARY ARE

a plank for a reach-board, a good barrel and a small piece
of 2 x 4 inch or 4 x 4 inch timber, or some pieces of one-
inch plank which may be nailed together to make 4-inch
stuff. Select a good, sound stave and rest it upon a block of
4 x 4 inch timber so that the center line of the block is parallel with the bowstring line of the stave (P R, Fig. 17), and
so that the outside edge of the stave cuts the corner of the
block at D (Fig. 14), as shown by Fig. 13; then with a soft
pencil or a sharp-pointed nail draw an outline of the stave
on the wood, and with a rule or straight-edged piece of
plank continue the outside line to the end of the block (A,
Fig. 14). Take another stave for the bottom of the toboggan and place it so that the end extends upon the block to
the line C C (Fig. 14) and the outside edge of the stave
reaches the corner B just as the first stave reached the corner D. with your straight-edge continue the line B B to the
edge of the block as you did in the first place with the line
A D. this will give you a block marked as in Fig. 14. Now
saw down through the line C C until you reach the lower
outline D E of the upper stave; next begin at D and saw
down to E. this will cut out C E D and leave Fig. 15.

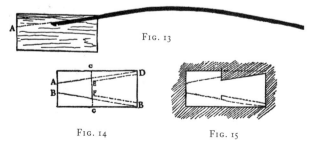

FIG. 13

FIG. 14

FIG. 15

Saw Along the Line

A until you cut off the block A C as shown in Fig. 18. This, as you see, leaves a place for the stave to fit. In the

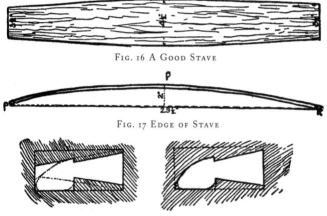

Fig. 16 A Good Stave

Fig. 17 Edge of Stave

Fig. 18 and 19 Evolution of Blocks

same manner cut out the block C B of Fig. 14 as shown in Fig. 18. Now take your blue pencil again and sketch the bow of the sled-runner as shown by the dotted lines (Fig. 18). Saw off the pieces to correspond with these lines, and after trimming away the angles with a sharp knife or chisel you will have the end piece (Fig. 19). You can probably make this piece in less time than it takes me to tell you how to do it.

If the Lumber at Hand

is 2 x 4 inches make duplicate pieces of the shape shown in Fig. 19 and nail these together, making one piece 4 inches across the base. The average barrel stave (Fig. 16 and 17) is about 4 or 5 inches across the middle,

3½ to 4 inches or more in width at the two ends, and about 29½ inches long measured on a straight line from end to end—that is, if the curved stave is thought of as a bow, the bowstring would be 29½ inches long and the arch about 2 inches high between the middle of the string and the outside of the bow (Fig. 17).

When making

THE STERN BLOCKS

to the runners cut both sides as the top is cut in Fig. 18; then it is necessary only to round off the ends as in Figs. 20 and 21.

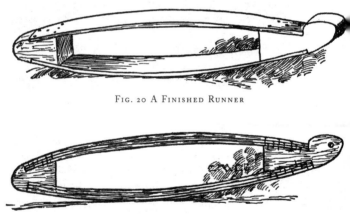

FIG. 20 A FINISHED RUNNER

FIG. 21 A REINFORCED RUNNER

If the barrels you have are of too light material to support the weight they must carry, this defect is easily remedied by cutting deeper notches in the blocks so that two or three staves together instead of single ones may be used for the upper and under side of the runner (Fig. 21).

Each toboggan may be made of two runners (Fig. 22), or

A Third Runner

may be put in the middle, making it almost the same as a solid board for both top and bottom. Remember that the broad piece of board which represents

The Top of the Toboggan

(Fig. 22) must be nailed on from the under side; consequently this work must be done before the lower runners are nailed on the bow and stern blocks, and the top boards

THE STAVE TOBOGGAN

Fig. 22 Showing construction of two runners

must set a little back of the centers of the sledges. Fig. 21 represents the rear toboggan of the bob; the front toboggan differs from the rear one in having a longer projecting cross-piece at the bow ends to be used as a foot-rest and to help in steering (Figs. 32, 33, and 34). In making

A LIGHT TOBOGGAN-BOB

it is not necessary to build it on the elaborate plan shown in Figs. 32, 33 and 34; in fact, the top board of the toboggan may be simply nailed fast to the reach-board (see Fig. 23, p. 257), while the bow-axle can be arranged by fastening to the reach-board a block shaped like that shown in Fig. 30, and then dropping a bolt through a hole in the reach-board, through a hole in the center of the block, and through another hole bored in the top pieces of the bow toboggan (Figs. 30 and 31). Fig. 24 shows

A WELL-MADE FRONT AXLE

bolted through the top board and the top staves with iron bolts and fastened to the reach-board by a king bolt secured with a nut at the lower end.

Figs. 25 and 26 show how to make

THE REAR-AXLE BLOCKS

such as are used in Figs. 32 and 34, but these may be simplified in a light toboggan by making half-round notches in the blocks (Figs. 27 and 28), and using a wooden axle (Fig. 29). This axle is secured to the axle-blocks by nailing a piece of an old trunk-strap over the axle and to the axle-block (Fig. 27) and securing it by two other straps nailed to the reach-board and axle-block, so as to cross the first strap at right angles and

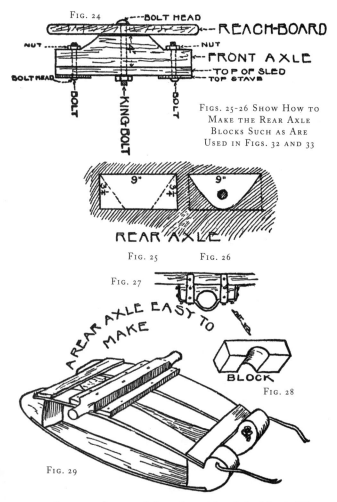

FIG. 24 —BOLT HEAD

NUT —— —— NUT

BOLT HEAD

FIGS. 25-26 SHOW HOW TO
MAKE THE REAR AXLE
BLOCKS SUCH AS ARE
USED IN FIGS. 32 AND 33

REACH-BOARD

FRONT AXLE

TOP OF SLED
TOP STAVE

BOLT · KING·BOLT · BOLT

REAR AXLE

FIG. 25   FIG. 26

FIG. 27

A REAR AXLE EASY TO MAKE

BLOCK

FIG. 28

FIG. 29

extend over and around the other side of the block (Fig. 27). This will allow a free up-and-down movement of the rear toboggan and prevent sudden jolts. A line, a rope, or a chain should be run from the front pieces of the rear toboggan and fastened to screw-eyes on the under side of the reach board (Fig. 32) to prevent the rear toboggan's turning from side to side.

THE KING BOLT

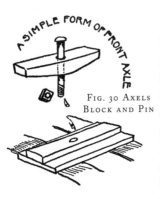

FIG. 30 AXELS BLOCK AND PIN

FIG. 31 LOWER AXEL BLOCK

is the only part of either of these two simple toboggan-bobs which may have to be bought at a shop; the rest of the material can be found around any country or suburban house. But if the reader is ambitious to make a more pretentious affair he may construct the front and rear axles as shown in Figs. 24, 25, 26 and 32.

THE FRONT AXLES

have already been described; after the rear-axle blocks are securely nailed or screwed to the under side of the reach-board and flush with its edges, an iron bolt is run through a block which has been previously bolted to the top of the stern toboggan, as shown by the dotted lines in Figs. 24 and 32.

By reference to this diagram you will see the ropes attached to the stern toboggan

TO PREVENT ITS SHEERING

from one side to the other and wrenching loose from the reach-board, while the axle pieces moving freely upon the iron bolt allow the toboggan to move up and down over the uneven places in the hill-side. The front axle allows free movement from one side to the other to guide the craft. The toboggan may be steered as shown in Fig. 33, the pilot sitting upright on the top piece, or he may lie prone upon the reach-board, grasp the ends of the foot-rest with his hands, and then steer by a movement of the arms.

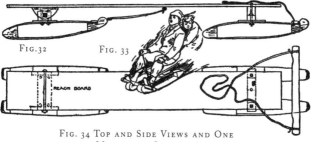

Fig. 32   Fig. 33

Fig. 34 Top and Side Views and One
Method of Steering

If you place the boards upon which the axles rest a little back of the center of the toboggan it will

Elevate the Bows
of the Runners,

thus making it easier for them to overcome obstructions, and will do away with the danger of burying the runners in any accidental mound or lump of snow that may be found in the road.

The toboggans may be used without the reach-board as ordinary sleds (Fig. 23), but before using them the

Fig. 23 Showing How it May Be Used as a Sled

runners should be smoothed with sandpaper or rubbed with an old soft brick and coated with oil or tallow.

AN OBVIOUS ADVANTAGE

of these barrel-stave toboggans, one which adds greatly to the comfort of the coasters when sliding over an uneven surface, is that the runner itself is a spring.

Boys know well how often they are obliged to give up their sledding and coasting because the snow is not just right for it. This is not so bad when it happens during the school-term, for there is little enough time then for outdoor sports. But when the holidays come, and the snow then is light and flaky, and refuses to pack, or there is only a thin crust so that their sleds break through—then it is that boys wish they could manage the weather themselves and order their own kind of snow. In default of this, however, there is one thing they can do: make such a toboggan-bob as I have described here. It is fairly simple to make, it can be used on snow that is too deep or too soft for a narrow-runner sled, and it is perfectly safe on a steep hill which would be dangerous to coast down on an ordinary sled. And when summer comes it may be used to coast down grassy hill-sides.

3.
How to Make Plain Sledsand Bob-sleighs

*T*HE sled with high runners looks odd to a Yankee, but it has its advantages when the snow is soft and deep, and it may be for this reason that the runners of

THE NATIVE SLEDS
OF THE OHIO VALLEY

average more inches in height than the sled runners of New England, where the snow is seldom slush as it is further south. Anyone can make the Ohio sled who has access to a lumber pile, a saw, a hammer and some nails. From the inch pine board 1, 2, 7, 6 (Fig. 35) saw off the triangles 1, 2, 3 and 5, 6, 7, then with your jack-knife round off the corners at 1 and 3 as shown in the diagram (Fig. 35).

A few inches from the stern, saw two slits one inch deep and 2 inches apart, then knock out the block, leaving a rectangular notch 1 inch deep by 2 inches broad (see 8 or Fig. 35); trim it evenly with your jack-knife and make a duplicate notch near the bow of the runner (9, Fig. 35); these are to hold the ends of the two braces shown in the diagram (Fig. 35). Lay the runner on another inch pine board and trace its outline, then make the duplicate runner in the same manner that you did the first. Now take two strips 1 inch by 2 inches, and about 15 inches long, fit them in the notches so that the runners will stand about 1 foot apart (Fig. 35); see that

THE OHIO SLED
ONE ANY ONE CAN MAKE

FIG. 36

FIG. 35

the ends of the braces are flush with the outside of the right-hand runner and fasten them securely in place with nails or screws, after which saw the protruding ends of the braces even with the outside of the left-hand runner. Next hunt up a piece of board long and wide enough for a top; cut it as shown in Fig. 36, and nail it to the runners, and the sled is finished.

To make it run smoothly the runners should be shod with iron; narrow strips of sheet-iron will answer the purpose, but half-round iron is the ideal thing.

On a short sled the half-round irons will be sufficiently secure if fastened only at the bow and stern of each runner, as shown in the diagram of the bob (Figs. 40, 43, and 45). The Ohio sled may be made of rough lumber, or it may be made of good planed wood and finished in the most elegant style.

In "the good old days" if have seen such sleds 7 and 8 feet long, loaded underneath with *pit-iron* to give weight and velocity.

If you desire to further test your ability by building something more difficult than a simple Ohio sled, you may try your hand in the construction of

A DOUBLE RUNNER, TRAVERSE OR BOB-SLEIGH

as it is variously called in different localities. When skillfully built, one of these compound sleds is enough of an achievement to satisfy the vaulting ambition of even an amateur carpenter. The bob-sleigh is made by joining with a reach-board two low-runnered sleds or "bobs."

Almost any sort of tough wood will answer for the purpose, but since we are going to spend time and skill upon this work we will select good, strong 1¼-inch oak planks for the runners. We shall need four pieces of the oak plank, each 5 inches broad by 32 inches long (A B D C, Fig. 37). From the end of one of these pieces (A) measure 5 inches (to E), and mark the point; from the opposite end (at B) measure 8 inches (to G) and mark the point; from E and G measure 2 inches toward the middle of the plank and mark the points H and K. Now take a carpenter's pencil, or a blue pencil, and rule with a straight-edge the line H J K (see dotted line on Fig. 37); also rule the lines GK, FJ, EH and HC. On the lower edge of the plank, 10 inches from D, on the line DC, mark the point L. on the line BD, 1 inch below B, mark the point P; also on the same line, 1½ inches above D, mark the point N, and on line BA, 1½ inches from B, mark b, and draw the lines LN, MP and Kb.

The pencil lines which you have drawn will now show a rough outline of a sled runner (C H J K b B P L, Fig. 37). Round off the angles by sketching inside of the ruled lines the curved lines of the bow of the runner, as shown in Fig. 37.

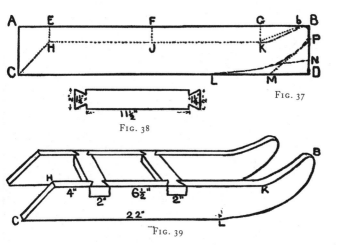

Fig. 37

Fig. 38

Fig. 39

The Contruction of a Bob

Saw slits from G to K, F to J and E to H; then cut out the block A E H C by sawing along the line CH until you meet the slit at H. it is now an easy matter to saw along the line from H to K and from b to K, which removes the pieces E H J F, F J K G AND G K b, leaving us only the triangle P M D and the small piece made by the line LN crossing MP to be sawed off the lower edge of the runner.

When all the saw work is done, the angles may be rounded with plane, chisel or jack-knife to conform to the sketched lines of the prow of the runner. Using the runner just finished as a pattern, make each of the other three exactly like it.

The eight braces for the two bobs must now be cut from 1¼-inch oak. Make them 2 inches wide, 11½ inches long. At both ends of each brace make mortises to extend 1¼ inches, the width of the top runner (Figs. 38 and 39). Set each pair of runners upright on their bottom edges; lay the braces in place, then carefully trace the form of the mortises on the top edges of the runners, and with saw and chisel cut out the notches, as shown by Fig. 39. Fasten the braces securely in place with screws, and your two bobs only need top boards and half round iron shoes to finish them (see Figs. 40 and 43).

However, it takes two bobs and a reach-board to make a bob-sleigh, and so our work is really but half done.

THE REACH-BOARD

may be any length to suit your fancy; the one shown in the diagrams, Fig. 40 (side view) and Fig. 43 (top view) is 7 feet long, 11 inches wide and 1 inch thick, which makes a well-proportioned bob-sleigh.

There must be allowance for a certain amount of independent motion in the two bobs under the reach-board; this is provided for by the use of two iron pins, a horizontal one for the rear bob (see dotted lines, Figs. 40 and 43) and a vertical one for the front bob (Fig. 44).

For the rear bob take two pieces of 1½ inch oak, 9 x 3¾ inches (X, Fig. 41), saw off the corners as indicated by the dotted lines (Fig. 41), then round off the angles as in X, Fig. 40, where the right-hand piece is shown fastened to the under side of the reach-board. Between these two pin boards fit a 4 x 4 inch oak block, which must be bolted to the top of the bob (Y, Figs. 40 and 43, dotted lines); this block must be long enough to fit snugly between the pin boards and yet allow movement to the sled. Bore a hole through the block Y corresponding to holes bored in the pin boards X—this is for the horizontal iron pin.

The second pin block is also made of oak and securely bolted to the top of the front bob, as indicated by the dotted lines (Figs. 40, 44 and 43). In Fig. 44 is shown but half of the pin block, but as one half is a duplicate of the other, it was not thought necessary to draw both ends. The same liberty has been taken with the guard rail and reach braces in Fig. 43. As may be seen these are shown on the lower side of the diagram only. Fig. 42 shows the form of the reach braces, which are screwed securely to the under side of the reach-board and have an ash or hickory guard rail fastened to their ends, as shown in the lower part of Fig. 43.

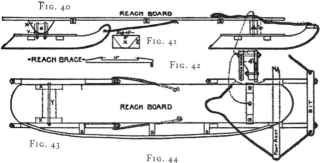

FIG. 44
PLAN, ELEVATION AND PARTS OF BOB-SLED

To prevent the stern bob from turning too far from side to side, ropes or chains are fastened from the bow ends of the rear runners to screw eyes on the under side of the reach-board.

A safe steering gear is the next important problem to solve and one can be made by an arrangement of a wooden bit, a foot rest or spreader and a pair of reins, as shown in Figs. 40 and 43. An iron pulley wheel should be securely fastened at each end of the spreader to hold the reins and facilitate the movement of the rope. The pulley wheel is not drawn in the diagram.

Figs. 45 and 46 show the details of a

Flushing Bob-Sleigh

Here you will notice that the pin block is set further back on the bow sled than it is in the one previously described; this is done to allow the driver to keep out of reach of his horse's heels. In other respects the bob-sleigh differs from the one shown in Figs. 40, 41, 42, 43 and 44, only in the addition of shafts for the horse and omission of steering apparatus. A stout plank is screwed fast across the front of the runners of the bow sled and a top brace bolted to it; the clips which hold the ends of the shafts are fastened to the top brace (Fig. 45).

This sort of bob-sleigh seems to be peculiar to Flushing. Moonlight nights when the sleighing is good the streets are alive with bobbing parties. If noise and laughter count as indications of fun, then is the

"Horse Bob"

truly a howling success. Many of them have two horses, hitched tandem, and the sport does not appear to be confined to very young people, for I have been on "bob

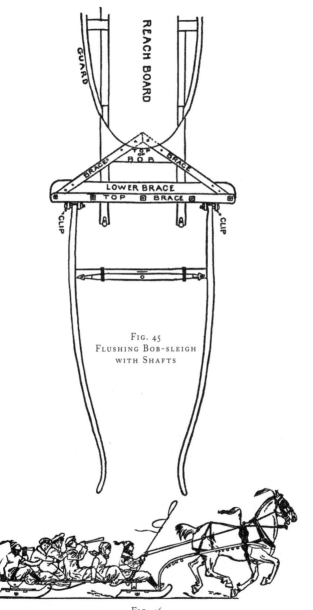

Fig. 45
Flushing Bob-sleigh
with Shafts

Fig. 46
The Flushing, L. I. Bob-sled

parties" where the frost was thicker and whiter in the hair of some of the merrymakers than it was on the ground over which they glided.

4.
The Van Kleeck Bob'

*T*HIS fast bob-sled is named after the Messrs. Van Kleeck, two gentlemen of Flushing, who own a double runner of this description which was built on their own designs, and is the swiftest bob-sled of my acquaintance.

It is neither so simple nor so crude as the rustic jumpers described some time ago, and it will test your skill to build it properly, but with all the plans and measurements before you the task should not be too difficult for even a boy who can handle tools.

THE SLEDS OF THE BOB'

are built entirely of good heavy oak; the runners of the sleds are 34¼ inches long, 4½ inches high, 1⅜ inches thick at the top, and ¾ of an inch thick at the bottom. To make the runners for the two sleds, one must have four ¾-inch oak planks, each 3 feet long by 5 or 6 inches wide. Trim these planks down to 4½ inches thick, by 34¼ inches long, and 4½ inches wide (Figs. 47 and 48). On the top of the runners measure 2½ inches from the stern toward the bow and draw a line to the bottom corner, then saw off the triangles. At a point about 8 inches from the bow end of one of the runners, mark a point from the beginning of the curve (Fig. 48), and describe a neat and gradual curve to the top of the bow end of the plank. Saw off a rough triangle first, and then trim down until the curve of the

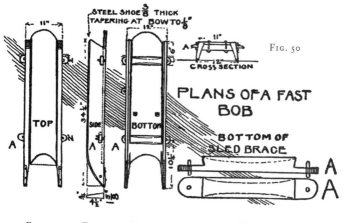

STEEL SHOE $\frac{3}{8}$" THICK
TAPERING AT BOW TO $\frac{1}{8}$"

FIG. 50

CROSS SECTION

PLANS OF A FAST
BOB

BOTTOM OF
SLED BRACE

A
A

TOP

SIDE

BOTTOM

FIG. 47   FIG. 48   FIG. 49   FIG. 51

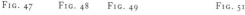

wood corresponds with the line drawn. Use this runner as a pattern and make the other three exactly like this one. The exact proportions are here given, not because others might not answer as well, but because this sled has proved to be a very fast one, and sleds, like boats, are fast or slow according to their lines and balance. After the runners are blocked out, trim them down on the inner sides with a plane until the lower edge is only ? of an inch broad (Fig. 48). The runners are set at an angle, as may be seen by Fig. 50, it being only 11 inches from outside to outside of top of sled, while it is 12 inches from out-side to outside of the bottom of the runners. There are two oak braces to each sled (Figs. 49, 50 and 51, AAA); these braces are 2 inches wide and 1½ inches thick, and cut with a beveled step or notch to fit the slant of the inside of the runners (Figs. 50 and 51). The top ends of the braces extend through holes cut for that purpose, 1½ inches beyond the outside of the runners, and ½ inch below the top edges of runners, and are held in place by oaken pegs or pins (Figs. 47, 48, 49, 50, 51). To make the parts fit exactly and to get the proportions correctly, it is best to make on tough wrapping paper a set of plans the exact size of the proposed sled, and use these patterns to test your work by constant comparison.

After the braces are made and found by experiment to fit the runners neatly, they may be rounded off on the under side, the better to pass over lumps of snow or ice which chance puts on the tracks.

Make the tops of the sleds of ½ inch oak planks according to the plans (Figs. 48, 49 and 50), to fit between the runners and rest upon the braces, which have been set ½ inch below tops of the runners purposely, to leave room for the top plank. Secure the top board to the braces by iron bolts with nuts screwed to the lower ends (Fig. 50).

The Reach-Board

should be of selected maple 10 feet long, 11 inches wide and 1 inch thick (Fig. 514). To it are bolted five oak braces, each 1½ inches wide by ¾ of an inch thick (B, Figs. 53, 54, and 55). The center of the bow-brace is 1½ feet astern of the bow of the reach-board, and the center of the stern-brace is 6 inches forward of the stern of the reach-board. The bow-brace is 1 foot 1 inch long, and the others are all 1 foot 3 inches in length. To the braces hickory hands or guard rails are bolted (Figs. 54 and 55), and the bow ends of the rails are fastened with large screws to the sides of the reach-board.

Thus far I have described only a well-made bob, but when we come to joining the reach-board to the sleds we use

The Van Kleeck Device,

which lets the bob over the "thank-you-marms" without the hard thud and jolt to which we are so accustomed.

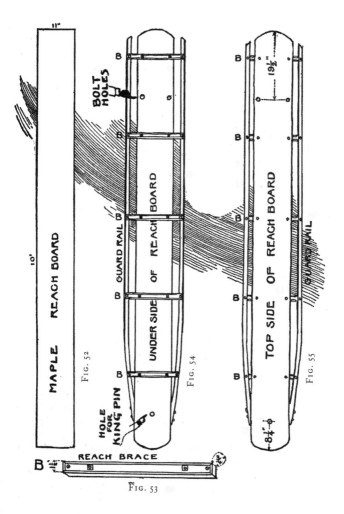

11"

10'

MAPLE   REACH BOARD

FIG. 52

BOLT HOLES

GUARD RAIL

UNDER SIDE   OF   REACH BOARD

FIG. 54

HOLE FOR KING PIN

19½"

TOP SIDE   OF   REACH BOARD

GUARD RAIL

FIG. 55

8¼"

B REACH BRACE

FIG. 53

Reference to Fig. 56 will show that, contrary to custom, the king bolt does not go through the top of the sled, but is fastened by two washers and two nuts to an oak block, and the block is itself bolted to the sled top by two iron knuckles; this arrangement not only allows the front sled to turn sidewise in any direction, but it can tip up and down, until the ends of the runners strike the reach-board, thus allowing the sled to adapt itself to the unevenness of the track without making heart-breaking jolts. Figs. 59, 61, and 62 will show you that the stern sled is similarly provided with knuckles, but in the latter case there is no king pin, the oaken blocks being respectively bolted to the reach-board and the stern sled.

Where the king pin goes through the reach-board there is an oak block 10¾ inches long, 4½ inches wide and a trifle over 1 inch thick, bolted across the bottom of the reach-board; to this is screwed an iron plate; another and longer iron plate is screwed to the big oak block below, and an iron washer separates the two (Figs. 56 and 57) and lessens the friction. The plate on the big block is not screwed on until the nuts for the knuckle bolts are let into the holes cut for them and the knuckle bolts screwed into the nuts (see dotted lines, Figs. 56 and 57).

Across the tops of the sled is another oaken piece, ½ inch thick, 4½ inches wide and 11 inches long, and

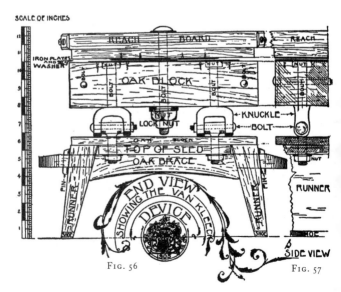

FIG. 56

FIG. 57

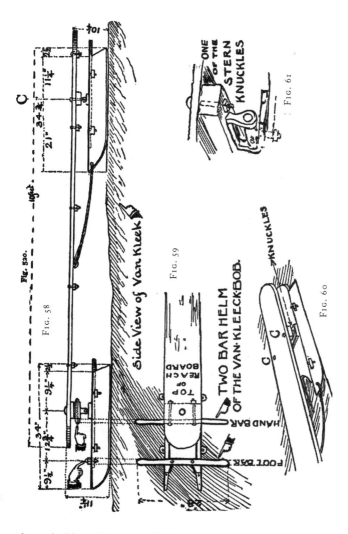

Fig. 58

Fig. 52a.

Side View of Van Kleek

Fig. 59

TWO BAR HELM
OF THE VAN-KLEECKBOB.

TOP OF REACH BOARD.

HAND BAR

FOOT BAR

Fig. 60

KNUCKLES

C

ONE OF THE STERN KNUCKLES

Fig. 61

through this and the top of the sled the lower bolts of the knuckles pass, and are held in place below by nuts and washers. The runners of the sleds are shod with steel bands ⅜ of an inch thick and tapering gradually at the bow to ⅛ of an inch, where it overlaps and is screwed on top of runner. Of course the hardware must be made by a smith.

THE STEERING APPARATUS

REGULAR
USE OF THE TWO
BARS

FIG. 62

can best be understood by examining Figs. 58 and 59, where it will be seen that there is a solid oak foot-bar bolted across the bow of the sled, its center 9½ inches from the points of the runners, and a stout hickory hand-bar bolted to the bog oaken block below the reach-board. Fig. 62 shows the proper way to steer a heavily loaded bob down a steep hill.

This steering apparatus is simple, safe and effective, and the pilot has the full strength or arms and legs available for turning the bow-sled as occasion requires. Fig. 63 shows the construction of an iron bob brake, and Figs. 64, 65, 66 and 67, the parts of a wooden brake, with teeth or iron bolts.

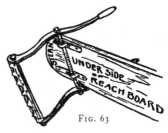

UNDER SIDE
REACH BOARD

FIG. 63

Before using your racing bob polish the steel shoes with emery cloth until they are as smooth as it is possible to make them, and then oil them with sweet oil; thus prepared, the heavy bob will slip down so quickly as to explain why one man calls his "The Oyster."

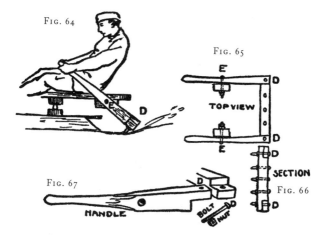

FIG. 64

FIG. 65

E

D

TOP VIEW

D

E

D

SECTION

FIG. 66

D

FIG. 67

D

HANDLE

BOLT

NUT

How to Steer a Bob-sled

*O*F late there has been a great revival of interest among people of all ages in the boyish sport of coasting and tobogganing. So keen has this become that we find in Europe clubs formed for coasting down the mountain side, and tracks built in deep snows with many difficult twists and turns to test the skill of the pilots on the American bobs, which they use and which are there improperly called toboggans. Also some of the New York papers have been filed with letters from bald-headed and gray-headed "boys" discussing propriety of certain terms familiar to their youthful days and used in connection with the different methods of steering their sleds or bobs down the snowy hillside. But we will not enter into this discussion, for the good reason that the terms in question, "belly-buster," "belly-whopper," etc., are the ones used by the boys in different sections of the country, and consequently all of them proper in describing the method of coasting where the coaster lies prone upon the sled and goes down head first; but with the improvement of the sled and the bob there have crept in a number of devices for steering these crafts, the use of which

SHOULD BE FORBIDDEN BY THE AUTHORITIES

because of the imminent peril the riders incur (especially the helmsman) when they are used.

There are almost as many methods of steering as there are styles of sled.

Some people crowd on the sled with

LEGS EXTENDED ON EACH SIDE

and steer or attempt to steer with sticks held in their hands. Others steer by sitting on the front of the sled and

VIGOROUSLY KICKING THEIR HEELS

upon the surface of the track as they go rushing down the hillside. This was the popular method in the Southwest, along the Ohio River, when the writer was a small boy, and many legs and arms were broken as a direct consequence of this style of steering. Another popular method in steering a small sled was to

SIT SIDEWAYS ON ONE LEG

and allow the other leg to dangle out behind with the foot resting on the surface of the snow. This style of steering I have seen used by the tobogganers on Mt. Royal, up in Canada. It is comparatively safe for small sleds and toboggans, but when the foot is encased only in a moccasin it sometimes receives painful injuries in going down the steep courses, and I have noticed many bloody moccasins on the feet of our enthusiastic sport-loving Canadian brothers.

Belly-buster

Figs. 78 and 79 show the coaster going down head first. This is an exciting and exhilarating manner of coasting, but should never be used on dangerous courses where there is any liability of the coaster's head striking something harder than a soft snow bank; but on safe hills there can be no serious objection to coasting head first, unless it be that the sport itself is always strenuous and dangerous enough without unnecessarily adding to this element.

The Wheel

(Figs. 68 and 69) which is in common use, leaves no avenue of escape for the pilot; in case of accident he will be jammed suddenly and with great force against the iron wheel and the inflexible iron upright bar, which can but produce the most serious results.

The Wheel Helm

is composed of an iron wheel fastened to an iron rod which has a "squared" head fitting into a square hole in the hub of the wheel (Figs. 68 and 69); this arrangement causes the rod to turn with every turn of the wheel; the lower end of the wheel rod is also "squared" to fit into

Fig. 68

Fig. 69

Fig. 70

Fig. 71

DANGEROUS STEERING GEAR

the oaken block, which is bolted to the front sled of the bob; thus it may be seen that every turn of the wheel also turns the sled—an excellent plan *if no one had to sit behind and astride of the shaft of the wheel.*

Built on the same principle as the wheel helm, Figs. 70 (cross section, front elevation) and 71 should never be used, for any sort of iron or wooden steering apparatus which extends above the reach-board contains possibilities of serious or even fatal results to the coasters. Rather than use either of the foregoing helms it is better to abandon all steering appliances and depend upon your unaided hands to control the direction of the front sled—a method often resorted to by small boys, who stretch their bodies full length upon the reach-board and grasp with their hands the front of the runners of the bow-sled (Fig. 72), or the back part of the same runners (Fig. 73), and dart head first down the ice-coated hills.

The positions shown by Figs. 73 and 72 are those which all boys know under the forceful but eloquent names of "belly-buster," "belly-whopper," or "belly-gut." I will not stop to apologize for the use of these words, for they are now recognized as technical terms, and so used. But when one goes

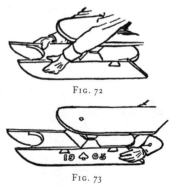

Fig. 72

Fig. 73

belly-buster, one leaves but little room for other passengers on the reach-board, and thus loses half the fun of coasting. One of the best ways to steer a loaded bob is with

FIG. 74

FIG. 75

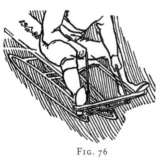

FIG. 76

CROSSED LINES

as shown by Figs. 74 and 75. Fig. 75 shows a Yankee boy's way of using the crossed lines and feet without the aid of a foot-bar, while Fig. 76 shows an immovable iron foot-bar attached to the reach-board. In the last device the lines cross beneath the foot-bar, pass through smooth eyelets in the foot-bar and sometimes end in rings for the hands to grasp. The advantage of the crossed lines is apparent at a glance; it would be most difficult, indeed often impossible, to turn the sled by a direct pull, but when the line runs diagonally, a slight tug is sufficient to deflect the bow-sled.

Fig. 77 shows the bow-sled with a stout foot-bar bolted to it and extending half a foot on each side of the runners. With your feet on the foot-rest and the reins in your hands you can brace your foot firmly against one end of the bar as you pull on the proper rein with your hand; this gives the strength of one leg and one arm to each pull.

Fortunately for us all the long solid-runner sleds are now obsolete and no longer to be seen crowded with reckless men and boys whooping down the hill. These "leg-breakers" were guided by the man in front, who vigorously kicked the

FIG. 77

snow to the right or left as required. Small single sleds are to this day often guided in the same manner, but not with the same risk to life and limb.

While Figs. 75, 76 and 77 are all good methods to use, a better one still is to have a foot-bar on the bow of the front sled and a handle-bar attached to the king pin block of the same sled (Figs. 78 and 79). With this double helm it is an easy matter for the pilot to sit in the front of the reach-board with his feet upon the foot-bar

FIG. 78

FIG. 79

and his hands down at his sides grasping the hand-bar on each side of the reach-board (see Fig. 62). In this manner he can use all the force of the muscles in both legs and arms to guide the bob-sled. This is the Van Kleeck method.

When I said that the American bobs in Switzerland were called toboggans it is to be understood that I mean they are so called by the Americans, for it seems that the native Swiss call their rudely fashioned sled a *hand-schlitten* and their double runner a *luge*. At the celebrated Cred d'y Bau run at Caux the *luge* seems to be a term used for almost any form of sled, and coasting down these mountains is called *lugeing*. There are several of these coasting places in Switzerland, one of them five miles long. There is one at St. Montz called the Cresta which is only three and four-tenths miles long, but the coasters cover the distance in seventy-three seconds. Another place is at the Grindinwold, and all of the American methods of steering or guiding bobs are used at these places. But it is not necessary for Americans to go to Switzerland to find mountain sides upon which to coast. There are numerous places within reach of New York, not farther from Manhattan than Tuxedo, which might be used by enthusiastic lovers of the sport, and which would afford long and steep enough courses to satisfy the most enthusiastic dare-devil sportsman. Our own Rockies in the Northwest are buried in snow each year, and adventurous spirits can find on their steep declivities places to test their nerve and skill; but whatever course they slide or whatever the location of the hill, let them use common sense and abandon all steering gear which projects above the front of the reach-board, so that when they start down hill they may not only enjoy the coasting but be reasonable certain of reaching the bottom safely, thus making the ride enjoyable from the beginning to

THE END

SNAP-DRAGONS
A Tale of Christmas Eve
by *Juliana Horatia Ewing*

Mr. and Mrs. Skratdj

ONCE upon a time there lived a certain family of the name Skratdj. (It has a Russian or Polish look, and yet they most certainly lived in America.) They were remarkable for the following peculiarity. They seldom seriously quarreled, but they never agreed about anything. It is hard to say whether it were more painful for their friends to  hear them constantly contradicting each other, or gratifying to discover that it "meant nothing," and was "only their way."

It began with the father and mother. They were a worthy couple, and really attached to each other. But

they had a habit of contradicting each other's statements, and opposing each other's opinions, which,
though mutually understood and allowed for in private,
was most trying to the by-standers in public. If one
related an anecdote, the other would break in with half-
a-dozen corrections of trivial details of no interest or
importance to anyone, the speakers included. For
instance: Suppose the two dining in a strange house,
and Mrs. Skratdj seated by the host, and contributing to
the small-talk of the dinner-table. Thus:—

"Oh yes. Very changeable weather indeed. It
looked quite promising yesterday morning in the town,
but it began to rain at noon."

"A quarter past eleven, my dear," Mr. Skratdj's
voice would be heard to say from several chairs down,
in the corrective tones of a husband and a father; "and
really, my dear, so far from being a promising morning,
I must say it looked about as threatening as it well
could. Your memory is not always accurate in small matters, my love."

But Mrs. Skratdj had not been a wife and a mother
for fifteen years, to be snuffed out at one snap of the
marital snuffers. As Mr. Skratdj leaned forward in his
chair, she leaned forward in hers, and defended herself
across the intervening couples.

"Why, my dear Mr. Skratdj, you said yourself the
weather had not been so promising for a week."

"What I said, my dear, pardon me, was that the
barometer was higher than it had been for a week. But,
as you might have observed if these details were in your
line, my love, which they are not, the rise was extraor-
dinarily rapid, and there is no surer sign of unsettled
weather.—But Mrs. Skratdj is apt to forget these unim-
portant trifles," he added, with a comprehensive smile
round the dinner-table; "her thoughts are very properly

absorbed by the more important domestic questions of the nursery."

"Now I think that's rather unfair on Mr. Skratdj's part,"Mrs. Skratdj would chirp, with a smile quite as affable and as general as her husband's. "I'm sure he's *quite* as forgetful and inaccurate as *I* am. And I don't think *my* memory is at *all* a bad one."

"You forgot the dinner hour when we were going out to dine last week, nevertheless,"said Mr. Skratdj.

"And you couldn't help me when I asked you,"was the sprightly retort. "And I'm sure it's not like you to forget anything about *dinner*, my dear."

"The letter was addressed to you,"said Mr. Skratdj.

"I sent it to you by Jemima,"said Mrs. Skratdj.

"I didn't read it,"said Mr. Skratdj.

"Well, you burnt it,"said Mrs. Skratdj; "and, as I always say, there's nothing more foolish than burning a letter of invitation before the day, for one is certain to forget."

"I've no doubt you always do say it,"Mr. Skratdj remarked with a smile, "but I certainly never remember to have heard the observation from your lips, my love."

"Whose memory's in fault there?"asked Mrs. Skratdj triumphantly; and as at this point the ladies rose, Mrs. Skratdj had the last word.

Indeed, as may be gathered from this conversation, Mrs. Skratdj was quite able to defend herself. When she was yet a bride, and young and timid, she used to collapse when Mr. Skratdj contradicted her statements, and set her stories straight in public. Then she hardly ever opened her lips without disappearing under the domestic extinguisher. But in the course of fifteen years she had learned that Mr. Skratdj's bark was a great deal worse than his bite. (If, indeed, he had a bite at all.) Thus snubs that made other people's ears tingle, had no effect whatever on the lady to whom they were addressed, for she knew exactly what they were worth, and had by this time become fairly adept at snapping in return. In the days when she succumbed she was occasionally unhappy, but now she and her husband understood each other, and having agreed to differ, they unfortunately agreed also to differ in public.

Indeed, it was the by-standers who had the worst of it on these occasions. To the worthy couple themselves the habit had become second nature, and in no way affected the friendly tenour of their domestic relations. They would interfere with each other's conversation, contradicting assertions, and disputing conclusions for a whole evening; and then, when all the world and his wife thought that these ceaseless sparks of bickering must blaze up into a flaming quarrel as soon as they were alone, they would bowl amicably home in a cab, criticizing the friends who were commenting upon them, and as little agreed about the events of the evening s about the details of any other events whatever.

Yes. The by-standers certainly had the worst of it. Those who were near wished themselves anywhere else, especially when appealed to. Those who were at a distance did not mind so much. A domestic squabble at a certain distance is interesting, like an engagement viewed from a point beyond the range of guns. In such a position one may some day be placed oneself! Moreover, it gives a touch of excitement to a dull evening to be able to say *sotto voce* to one's neighbor, "Do listen! The Skratdjs are at it again!" Their unmarried friends thought a terrible abyss of tyranny and aggravation must lie beneath it all, and blessed their stars that they were still single, and able to tell a tale their own way. The married ones had more idea of how it really was, and wished in the name of common sense and good taste that Skratdj and his wife would not make fools of themselves.

So it went on, however; and so, I suppose, it goes on still, for not many bad habits are cured in middle age.

On certain questions of comparative speaking their views were never identical. Such as the temperature being hot or cold, things being light or dark, the apple-tarts being sweet or sour. So one day Mr. Skratdj came into the room, rubbing his hands, and planting himself at the fire with "Bitterly cold it is today, to be sure."

"Why, my dear William," said Mrs. Skratdj, "I'm sure you must have got a cold; a feel a fire quite oppressive myself."

"You were wishing you'd a seal-skin jacket yesterday, when it wasn't half as cold as it is today," said Mr. Skratdj.

"My dear William! Why, the children were shivering the whole day, and the wind was in the north."

"Due east, Mrs. Skratdj."

"I know by the smoke," said Mrs. Skratdj, softly but decidedly.

"I fancy I can tell an east wind when I feel it," said Mr. Skratdj, jocosely, to the company.

"I told Jemima to look at the weathercock," murmured Mrs. Skratdj.

"I don't care a fig for Jemima," said her husband.

On another occasion Mrs. Skratdj and a lady friend were conversing.

. . . "We met him at the Smiths'—a gentlemanlike agreeable man, about forty," said Mrs. Skratdj, in reference to some matter interesting to both ladies.

"Not a day over thirty-five," said Mr. Skratdj, from behind his newspaper.

"Why, my dear William, his hair's grey." Said Mrs. Skratdj.

"Plenty of men are grey at thirty," said Mr. Skratdj. "I knew a man who was grey at twenty-five."

"Well, forty or thirty-five, it doesn't much matter," said Mrs. Skratdj, about to resume her narration.

"Five years matter a good deal to most people at thirty-five," said Mr. Skratdj, as he walked towards the door. "They would make a remarkable difference to me, I know;" and with a jocular air Mr. Skratdj departed, and Mrs. Skratdj had the rest of the anecdote her own way.

THE LITTLE SKRATDJS

THE Spirit of Contradiction finds a place in most nurseries, though to a very varying degree in different ones. Children snap and snarl by nature, like young puppies; and most of us can remember taking part in some such spirited dialogues as the following:—

{ "I will."
  "You can't."

{ "You daren't."
  "I dare."

{ "You shall."
  "I won't."

{ "I'll tell Mamma."
  "I don't care if you do."

It is the part of wise parents to repress these squibs and crackers of juvenile contention, and to enforce that slowly-learned lesson, that in this world one must often "pass over" and "put up with" things in other people, being oneself by no means perfect. Also that it is a kindness, and almost a duty, to let people think and say and do things in their own way occasionally.

But even if Mr. and Mrs. Skratdj had ever thought of teaching all this to their children, it must be confessed that the lesson would not have come with a good grace from either of them, since they snapped and snarled between themselves as much or more than their children in the nursery.

The two eldest were the leaders in the nursery squabbles. Between these, a boy and a girl, a ceaseless war of words was waged from morning to night. And as neither of them lacked ready wit, and both were in constant practice, the art of snapping was cultivated by them to the highest pitch.

It began at breakfast, if not sooner.

"You've taken my chair."

"It's not your chair."

"You know it's the one I like, and it was in my place."

"How do you know it was in your place?"

"Never mind. I do know."

"No, you don't."

"Yes, I do."

"Suppose I say it was in my place."

"You can't, for it wasn't."

"I can, if I like."

"Well, was it?"

"I sha'n't tell you."

"Ah! That shews it wasn't"

"No, it doesn't."

"Yes, it does."

Etc., etc., etc.

The direction of their daily walks was a fruitful subject of difference of opinion.

"Let's go on the Common today, Nurse."

"Oh, don't let's go there; we're always going on the Common."

"I'm sure we're not. We've not been there for ever so long."

"Oh, what a story! We were there on Wednesday. Let's go down Gipsey Lane. We never go down Gipsey Lane."

"Why, we're always going down Gipsey Lane. And there's nothing to see there."

"I don't care. I won't go on the Common, and I shall go and get Papa to say we're to go down Gipsey Lane. I can run faster than you."

"That's very sneaking; but I don't care."

"Papa! Papa! Polly's called me a sneak."

"No, I didn't, Papa."

"You did."

"No, I didn't. I only said it was sneaking of you to say you'd run faster than me, and get Papa to say we were to go down Gipsey Lane."

"Then you did call him sneaking," said Mr. Skratdj. "And you're a very naughty ill-mannered little girl. You're getting very troublesome, Polly, and I shall have to send you to school, where you'll be kept in order. Go where your brother wishes at once."

For Polly and her brother had reached an age when it was convenient, if possible, to throw the blame of all nursery differences on Polly. In families where domestic discipline is rather fractious than firm, there comes a stage when the girls almost invariably go to the wall, because they will stand snubbing, and the boys will not. Domestic authority, like some other powers, is apt to be magnified on the weaker class. But Mr. Skratdj would not always listen to Harry.

"If you don't give it me back directly, I'll tell about your eating the two magnum-bonums in the kitchen garden on Sunday," and Master Harry on one occasion.

"Tell-tale tit!
Your tongue shall be slit,
And every dog in the town shall have a little bit,"

quoted his sister.

"Ah! You've called me a tell-tale. Now I'll go and tell Papa. You got into a fine scrape for calling me names the other day."

"Go, then! I don't care."

"You wouldn't like me to go, I know."

"You daren't. That's what it is."

"I dare."

"Then why don't you?"

"Oh, I am going; but you'll see what will be the end of it."

Polly however, had her own reasons for remaining stolid, and Harry started. But when he reached the landing he paused. Mr. Skratdj had especially announced that morning that he did not wish to be disturbed, and though he was a favorite, Harry had no desire to invade the dining-room at this crisis. So he returned to the nursery, and said with a magnanimous air, "I don't want to get you into a scrape, Polly. If you'll beg my pardon I won't go."

"I'm sure I sha'n't,"said Polly, who was equally well informed as to the position of affairs at head-quarters. "Go, if you dare."

"I won't if you want me not,"said Harry, discreetly waiving the question of apologies.

"But I'd rather you went,"said the obdurate Polly. "You're always telling tales. Go and tell now, if you're not afraid."

So Harry went. But at the bottom of the stairs he lingered again, and was meditating how to return with most credit to his dignity, when Polly's face appeared through the banisters, and Polly's sharp tongue goaded him on.

"Ah! I see you. You're stopping. You daren't go."

"I dare," said Harry; and at last he went.

As he turned the handle of the door, Mr. Skratdj turned round.

"Please, Papa—" Harry began.

"Get away with you!" cried Mr. Skratdj. "Didn't I tell you I was not to be disturbed this morning? What an extraor—"

But Harry had shut the door, and withdrawn precipitately.

Once outside, he returned to the nursery with dignified steps, and an air of apparent satisfaction, saying,

"You're to give me the bricks, please."

"Who says so?"

"Why, who should say so? Where have I been, pray?"

"I don't know, and I don't care."

"I've been to Papa. There!"

"Did he say I was to give up the bricks?"

"I've told you."

"No, you've not."

"I sha'n't tell you any more."

"Then I'll go to Papa and ask."

"Go by all means."

"I won't if you'll tell me truly."

"I sha'n't tell you anything. Go and ask, if you dare," and Harry, only too glad to have the tables turned.

Polly's expedition met with the same fate, and she attempted to cover her retreat in a similar manner.

"Ah! You didn't tell."

"I don't believe you asked Papa."

"Don't you? Very well!"

"Well, did you?"

"Never mind."

Etc., etc., etc.

Meanwhile Mr. Skratdj scolded Mrs. Skratdj for not keeping the children in better order. And Mrs. Skratdj said it was quite impossible to do so, when Mr. Skratdj spoilt Harry as he did, and weakened her (Mrs. Skratdj's) authority by constant interference.

Difference of sex gave point to many of these nursery squabbles, as it so often does to domestic broils.

"Boys never will do what they're asked,"Polly would complain.

"Girls ask such unreasonable things,"was Harry's retort.

"Not half so unreasonable as the things you ask."

"Ah! That's a different thing! Women have got to do what men tell them, whether it's reasonable or not."

"No, they've not!"said Polly. "At least, that's only husbands and wives."

"All women are inferior animals,"said Harry.

"Try ordering Mamma to do what you want, and see!"said Polly.

"Men have got to give orders, and women have to obey,"said Harry, falling back on the general principle. "And when I get a wife, I'll take care I make her do what I tell her. But you'll have to obey your husband when you get one."

"I won't have a husband, and then I can do as I like."

"Oh, won't you? You'll try to get one, I know. Girls always want to be married."

"I'm sure I don't know why,"said Polly; "they must have had enough of men if they have brothers."

And so they went on, *ad infinitum*, with ceaseless arguments that proved nothing and convinced nobody, and a continual stream of contradiction that just fell short of downright quarrelling.

Indeed, there was a kind of snapping even less near to a dispute than in the cases just mentioned. The little

Skratdjs, like some other children, were under the unfortunate delusion that it sounds clever to hear little boys and girls snap each other up with smart sayings, and old and rather vulgar play upon words, such as:

"I'll give you a Christmas box. Which ear will you have it on?"

"I won't stand it."

"Pray take a chair."

"You shall have it tomorrow."

"Tomorrow never comes."

And so if a visitor kindly began to talk to one of the children, another was sure to draw near and "take up" all the first child's answers, with smart comments, and catches that sounded as silly as they were tiresome and impertinent.

And ill-mannered as this was, Mr. and Mrs. Skratdj never put a stop to it. Indeed, it was only a caricature of what they did themselves. But they often said, "We can't think how it is the children are always squabbling!"

THE SKRATDJ'S DOG AND THE HOT-TEMPERED GENTLEMAN

IT is wonderful how the state of mind of a whole household is influenced by the heads of it. Mr. Skratdj was a very kind master, and Mrs. Skratdj was a very kind mistress, and yet their servants lived in a perpetual fever of irritability that just fell short of discontent. They jostled each other on the back stairs, and sharp things in the pantry, and kept up a perennial warfare on the subject of the duty of the sexes with the general manservant. They gave warning on the slightest provocation.

The very dog was infected by the snapping mania. He was not a brave dog, he was not a vicious dog, and no high-breeding sanctioned his pretensions to arrogance. But like his owners, he had contracted a bad habit, a trick, which made him the pest of all timid visitors, and indeed of all visitors whatsoever.

The moment anyone approached the house, on certain occasions when he was spoken to, and often in no traceable connection with any cause at all, Snap the mongrel would rush out, and bark in his little sharp voice—"Yap! Yap! Yap!" If the visitor made a stand, he would bound away sideways on his four little legs; but the moment the visitor went on his way again, Snap was at his heels—"Yap! Yap! Yap!" He barked at the milkman, the butcher's boy, and the baker, though he saw them every day. He never got used to the washerwoman, and she never got used to him. She said he "put her in mind of that there black dog in the Pilgrim's Progress." He sat at the gate in summer, and yapped at every vehicle and every pedestrian who ventured to pass on the high road. He never but once had the chance of barking at burglars; and then, though he barked long and loud, nobody got up, for they said, "It's only Snap's way." The Skratdjs lost a silver teapot, a Stilton cheese, and two electro christening mugs, on this occasion; and Mr. and Mrs. Skratdj dispute who it was who discouraged reliance on Snap's warning to the present day.

One Christmas time, a certain hot-tempered gentleman came to visit the Skratdjs. A tall, sandy, energetic young man, who carried his own bag from the railway. The bag had been crammed rather than packed, after the wont of bachelors; and you could see where the heel of a boot distended the leather, and where the bottle of shaving cream lay.

As he came up to the house, out came Snap as usual—"Yap! Yap! Yap!" Now the gentleman was very fond of dogs, and had borne this greeting some dozen of times from Snap, who for his part knew the visitor quite as well as the washerwoman, and rather better than the butcher's boy. The gentleman had good, sensible, well-behaved dogs of his own, and was greatly disgusted with Snap's conduct. Nevertheless he spoke friendly to him; and Snap, who had had many a bit from his plate, could not help stopping for a minute to lick his hand. But no sooner did the gentleman proceed on his way, than Snap flew at his heels in the usual fashion—

"Yap! Yap! Yap!"

On which the gentleman—being hot-tempered, and one of those people with whom it is (as they say) a word and a blow, and the blow first—made a dash at Snap, and Snap taking to his heels, the gentleman flung his carpet-bag after him. The bottle of shaving cream hit upon a stone and was smashed. The heel of the boot caught Snap on the back, and sent him squealing to the kitchen. And he never barked at that gentleman again.

If the gentleman disapproved of Snap's conduct, he still less liked the continual snapping of the Skratdj family themselves. He was an old friend of Mr. and Mrs. Skratdj, however, and knew that they were really happy together, and that it was only a bad habit which made them constantly contradict each other. It was in allusion to their real affection for each other, and their perpetual

disputing, that he called them the "Snapping Turtles."

When the war of words waxed hottest at the dinner table between his host and hostess, he would drive his hands through his shock of sandy hair, and say, with a comical glance out of his umber eyes, "Don't flirt, my friends. It makes a bachelor feel awkward."

And neither Mr. nor Mrs. Skratdj could help laughing.

With the little Skratdjs his measures were more vigorous. He was very fond of children, and a good friend to them. He grudged no time or trouble to help them in their games and projects, but he would not tolerate their snapping up each other's words in his presence. He was much more truly kind than many visitors, who think it polite to smile at the sauciness and forwardness which ignorant vanity leads children so often to "shew off" before strangers. These civil acquaintances only abuse both children and parents behind their backs, for the very bad habits which they help to encourage.

The hot-tempered gentleman's treatment of his young friends was very different. One day he was talking to Polly, and making some kind inquiries about her lessons, to which she was replying in a quiet and sensible fashion, when up came Master Harry, and began to display his wit by comments on the conversation, and by snapping at and contradicting his sister's remarks, to which she retorted; and the usual snap-dialogue went on as usual.

"Then you like music," said the hot-tempered gentleman.

"Yes, I like it very much," said Polly.

"Oh, do you?" Harry broke in. "Then what are you always crying over it for?"

"I'm not always crying over it."

"Yes, you are."

"No, I'm not. I only cry sometimes, when I stick fast."

"You music must be very sticky, for you're always stuck fast."

"Hold your tongue!" said the hot-tempered gentleman.

With what he imagined to be a very waggish air, Harry put out his tongue, and held it with his finger and thumb. It was unfortunate that he had not time to draw it in again before the hot-tempered gentleman gave him a stinging box on the ear, which brought his teeth rather sharply together on the tip of his tongue, which was bitten in consequence.

"It's no use *speaking*," said the hot-tempered gentleman, driving his hands through his hair.

* * *

Children are like dogs, they are very good judges of their real friends. Harry did not like the hot-tempered gentlemen a bit the less because he was obliged to respect and obey him; and all the children welcomed him boisterously when he arrived that Christmas which we have spoken of in connection with his attack on Snap.

It was on the morning of Christmas Eve that the china punch bowl was broken. Mr. Skratdj had a warm dispute with Mrs. Skratdj as to whether it had been kept in a safe place; after which both had a brisk encounter with the housemaid, who did not know how it happened; and she, flouncing down the back passage, kicked Snap; who forthwith flew at the gardener as he was bringing in the horse-radish for the beef; who stepping backwards trode upon the cat; who spit and swore, and went up the pump with her tail as big as a fox's brush.

To avoid this domestic scene, the hot-tempered gentleman withdrew to the breakfast-room and took up a newspaper. By-and-by, Haryy and Polly came in, and they were soon snapping comfortably over their own affairs in a corner.

The hot-tempered gentleman's umber eyes had been looking over the top of his newspaper at them for some time, before he called, "Harry, my boy!"

And Harry came up to him.

"Shew me your tongue, Harry," said he.

"What for?" said Harry; "you're not a doctor."

"Do as I tell you," said the hot-tempered gentleman; and as Harry saw his hand moving, he put his tongue out with all possible haste. The hot-tempered gentleman sighed. "Ah!" he said in depressed tones; "I thought so!—Polly, come and let me look at yours."

Polly, who had crept up during this process, now put out hers. But the hot-tempered gentleman looked gloomier still, and shook his head.

"What is it?"cried both the children. "What do you mean?"And they seized the tips of their tongues in their fingers, to feel for themselves.

But the hot-tempered gentleman went slowly out of the room without answering; passing his hands through his hair, and saying, "Ah! Hum!"and nodding with an air of grave foreboding.

Just as he crossed the threshold, he turned back, and put his head into the room. "Have you ever noticed that your tongues are growing pointed?"he asked.

"No!"cried the children with alarm. "Are they?"

"If ever you find them becoming forked,"said the gentleman in solemn tones, "let me know."

With which he departed, gravely shaking his head.

In the afternoon the children attacked him again.

"*Do* tell us what's the matter with our tongues."

"You were snapping and squabbling just as usual this morning," said the hot-tempered gentleman.

"Well, we forgot," said Polly. "We don't mean anything, you know. But never mind that now, please. Tell us about our tongues. What is going to happen to them?"

"I'm very much afraid," said the hot-tempered gentleman, in solemn measured tones, "that you are both of you—fast—going—to—the—"

"Dogs?" suggested Harry, who was learned in cant expressions.

"Dogs!" said the hot-tempered gentleman, driving his hands through his hair. "Bless your life, no! Nothing half so pleasant! (That is, unless all dogs were like Snap, which mercifully they are not.) No, my sad fear is, that you are both of you—rapidly—going—*to the Snap-Dragons!*"

And not another word would the hot-tempered gentleman say on the subject.

CHRISTMAS EVE

IN the course of a few hours Mr. and Mrs. Skratdj recovered their equanimity. The punch was brewed in a jug, and tasted quite as good as usual. The evening was very lively. There were a Christmas tree, Yule cakes, log, and candles, furmety, and snap-dragon after supper. When the company was tired of the tree, and had gained an appetite by the hard exercise of stretching to high branches, blowing out "dangerous" tapers, and cutting ribbon and pack-thread in all directions, supper came, with its welcome cakes and furmety and punch. And when furmety somewhat palled upon the taste (and it must be admitted to boast more sentiment than flavor as a Christmas dish), the Yule candles were blown out and both the spirits and the palates of the

party were stimulated by the mysterious and pungent pleasures of snap-dragon.

Then, as the hot-tempered gentleman warmed his coat-tails at the Yule-log, a grim smile stole over his features as he listened to the sounds in the room. In the darkness the blue flames leaped and danced, the raisins were snapped and snatched from hand to hand, scattering fragments of flame hither and thither. The children shouted as the fiery sweetmeats burnt away the mawkish taste of the furmety. Mr. Skratdj cried that they were spoiling the carpet; Mrs. Skratdj complained that he had spilled some brandy on her dress. Mr. Skratdj retorted that she should not wear dresses so susceptible of damage in the family circle. Mrs. Skratdj recalled an old speech of Mr. Skratdj on the subject of wearing one's nice things for the benefit of one's family and not reserving them for visitors. Mr. Skratdj remembered that Mrs. Skratdj's excuse for buying that particular dress when she did not need it, was her intention of keeping it for the next year. The children disputed as to the credit for courage and the amount of raisins due to each. Snap barked furiously at the flames; and the maids hustled each other for good places in the doorway, and would not have allowed the man-servant to see at all, but he looked over their heads.

"St! St! At it! At it!"chuckled the hot-tempered gentleman in undertones. And when he said this, it seemed as if the voices of Mr. and Mrs. Skratdj rose higher in matrimonial repartee, and the children's squabbles became louder, and the dog yelped as if he were mad, and the maids' contest was sharper; whilst the snap-dragon flames leaped up and up, and blue fire flew about the room like foam.

At last the raisins were finished, the flames were all but out, and the company withdrew to the drawing-room. Only Harry lingered.

"Come along, Harry,"said the hot-tempered gentleman.

"Wait a minute,"said Harry.

"You had better come,"said the gentleman.

"Why?"said Harry.

"There's nothing to stop for. The raisins are eaten, the brandy is burnt out—"

"No, it's not,"said Harry.

"Well, almost. It would be better if it were quiet out. Now come. It's dangerous for a boy like you to be alone with the Snap-Dragons tonight."

"Fiddle-sticks!"said Harry.

"Go your own way, then!"said the hot-tempered gentleman; and he bounced out of the room, and Harry was left alone.

DANCING WITH THE DRAGONS

HE crept up to the table, where one little pale blue flame flickered in the snap-dragon dish.

"What a pity it should go out!"said Harry. At this moment the brandy bottle on the side-board caught his eye.

"Just a little more," murmured Harry to himself; and he uncorked the bottle, and poured a little brandy on to the flame.

Now of course, as soon as the brandy touched the fire, all the brandy in the bottle blazed up at once, and the bottle split to pieces; and it was very fortunate for Harry that he did not get seriously hurt. A little of the hot brandy did get into his eyes, and made them smart, so that he had to shut them for a few seconds.

But when he opened them again, what a sight he saw! All over the room the blue flames leaped and danced as they had leaped and danced in the soup plate with the raisins. And Harry saw that each successive flame was the fold in the long body of a bright blue Dragon, which moved like the body of a snake. And the room was full of these Dragons. In the face they were like the dragons on e sees made of very old blue and white china; and they had forked tongues, like the tongues of serpents. They were most beautiful in color, being sky-blue. Lobsters who have just changed their coats are very handsome, but the violet and indigo of a lobster's coat is nothing to the brilliant sky-blue of a Snap-Dragon.

How they leaped about! They were for ever leaping over each other, like seals at play. But if it was "play" at all with them, it was of a very rough kind; for as they jumped, they snapped and barked at each other, and their barking was like that of the barking Gnu in the Zoological Gardens; and from time to time they tore the hair out of each other's heads with their claws, and scattered it about the floor. And as it dropped it was like the flecks of flame people shake from their fingers when they are eating snap-dragon raisins.

Harry stood aghast.

"What fun!" said a voice close by him, and he saw that one of the Dragons was lying near, and not joining in the game. He had lost one of the forks of his tongue by accident, and could not bark for awhile.

"I'm glad you think it funny," said Harry, "I don't."

"That's right. Snap away!" sneered the Dragon. "You're a perfect treasure. They'll take you in with them the third round."

"Not those creatures?" cried Harry.

"Yes, those creatures. And if I hadn't lost my bark, I'd be the first to lead you off," said the Dragon. "Oh the game will exactly suit you."

"What is it, please?" Harry asked.

"You'd better not say 'please' to the others," said the Dragon, "if you don't want to have all your hair pulled out. The game is this. You have always to be jumping over somebody else, and you must either talk or bark. If anybody speaks to you, you must snap in return. I need not explain what *snapping* is. *You know*. If anyone by accident gives a civil answer, a claw-full of hair is torn out of his head to stimulate his brain. Nothing can be funnier."

"I dare say it suits you capitally," said Harry; "but I'm sure we shouldn't like it. I mean men and women and children. It wouldn't do for us at all."

"Wouldn't it?" said the Dragon. "You don't know how many human beings dance with dragons on Christmas Eve. If we are kept going in a house till after midnight, we can pull people out of their beds, and take them to dance in Vesuvius."

"Vesuvius!" cried Harry.

"Yes, Vesuvius. We come from Italy originally, you know. Our skins are the color of the Bay of Naples. We live on dried grapes and ardent spirits. We have glorious fun in the mountain sometimes. Oh! What snapping, and scratching, and tearing! Delicious! There are times when the squabbling becomes too great, and Mother Mountain won't stand it, and spits us all out, and throws cinders after us. But this is only at times. We had a charming meeting last year. So many human beings, and how they *can* snap! It was a choice party. So very select. We always have plenty of saucy children, and servants. Husbands and wives too, and quite as many of the former as the latter, if not more. But besides these, we had two vestry-men, a country postmaster, who devoted his talents to insulting the public instead of to learning the postal regulations, three cabmen and two "fares," two young shop-girls from a Berlin wool shop in a town where there was no competition, four commercial travelers, six landladies, six Old Bailey lawyers, several widows from almshouses, seven single gentlemen and nine cats, who swore at everything; a dozen sulphur-colored screaming cockatoos; a lot of street children from a town; a pack of mongrel curs from the colonies, who snapped at the human beings' heels, and five elderly ladies in their Sunday bonnets with Prayer-books, who had been fighting for good seats in church."

"Dear me!" said Harry.

"If you can find nothing sharper to say than 'Dear me,'" said the Dragon, "you will fare badly, I can tell you. Why, I thought you'd a sharp tongue, but it's not forked yet, I see. Here they are, however. Off with you! And if you value your curls—Snap!

And before Harry could reply, the Snap-Dragons came on on their third round, and as they passed they swept Harry with them.

He shuddered as he looked at his companions. They were as transparent as shrimps, but of this lovely cerulaean blue. And as they leaped they barked— "Howf! Howf?"—like barking Gnus; and when they leaped Harry had to leap with them. Besides barking, they snapped and wrangled with each other; and in this Harry must join also.

"Pleasant, isn't it?" said one of the blue Dragons.

"Not at all," snapped Harry.

"That's your bad taste," snapped the blue Dragon.

"No, it's not!" snapped Harry.

"Then it's pride and perverseness. You want your

hair combing."

"Oh, please don't!" shrieked Harry, forgetting himself. On which the Dragon clawed a handful of hair out of his head, and Harry screamed, and the blue Dragons barked and dance.

"That made your hair curl, didn't it?" asked another Dragon, leaping over Harry.

"That's no business of yours," Harry snapped, as well as he could for crying.

"It's more my pleasure than business," retorted the Dragon.

"Keep it to yourself, the," snapped Harry.

"I mean to share it with you, when I get hold of your hair," snapped the Dragon.

"Wait till you get the chance," Harry snapped, with desperate presence of mind.

"Do you know whom you're talking to?" roared the Dragon; and he opened his mouth from ear to ear, and shot out his forked tongue in Harry's face; and the boy was so frightened that he forgot to snap, and cried pietously,

"Oh, I beg your pardon, please don't!"

On which the blue Dragon clawed another handful of hair out of his head, and all the Dragons barked as before.

How long the dreadful game went on Harry never exactly knew. Well practiced as he was in snapping in the nursery, he often failed to think of a retort, and paid for his unreadiness by the loss of his hair. Oh, how foolish and wearisome all this rudeness and snapping now seemed to him! But on he had to go, wondering all the time how near it was to twelve o'clock, and whether the Snap-Dragons would stay till midnight and take him with them to Vesuvius.

At last, to his joy, it became evident that the brandy

was coming to an end. The Dragons moved slower, they could not leap so high, and at last one after another they began to go out.

"Oh, if they only all of them get away before twelve!" thought poor Harry.

At last there was only one. He and Harry jumped about and snapped and barked, and Harry was thinking with joy that he was the last, when the clock in the hall gave that whirring sound which some clocks do before they strike, as if it were clearing its throat.

"Oh, *please* go!" screamed Harry in despair.

The blue Dragon leaped up, and took such a clawful of hair out of the boy's head, that it seemed as if part of the skin went too. But that leap was his last. He went out at once, vanishing before the first stroke of twelve. And Harry was left on his face on the floor in the darkness.

CONCLUSION

WHEN his friends found him there was blood on his forehead. Harry thought it was where the Dragon had clawed him, but they said it was a cut from a fragment of the broken brandy bottle. The Dragons had disappeared as completely as the brandy.

Harry was cured of snapping. He had had quite enough of it for a lifetime, and the catch-contradictions of the household now made him shudder. Polly had not had the benefit of his experiences, and yet she improved also.

In the first place, snapping, like other kinds of quarreling, requires two parties to it, and Harry would never be a party to snapping anymore. And when he gave civil and kind answers to Polly's smart speeches, she felt ashamed of herself, and did not repeat them.

In the second place, she heard about the Snap-Dragons. Harry told all about it to her and to the hot-tempered gentleman.

"No do you think it's true?" Polly asked the hot-tempered gentleman.

"Hum! Ha!" said he, driving his hands through his hair. "You know I warned you, you were going to the Snap-Dragons."

Harry and Polly snubbed "the little ones" when they snapped, and utterly discountenanced snapping in the nursery. The example and admonitions of elder children are a powerful instrument of nursery discipline, and before long there was not a "sharp tongue" amongst all the little Skratdjs.

But I doubt if the parents ever were cured. I don't know if they heard the story. Besides, bad habits are not easily cured when one is old.

I fear Mr. and Mrs. Skratdj have yet got to dance with the Dragons.

THE BEST WREATH EVER AND OTHER HANGING DECORATIONS

Soft Sculpture Holly Wreath

MATERIALS: ¼ yard red polka-dotted fabric; ⅔ yard green print fabric; 1 yard green polka-dotted fabric; 1½ pounds fiberfill; one 18-inch (diameter) plastic foam wreath (3 inches wide).

INSTRUCTIONS: Cut green polka-dotted fabric 8 by 58 inches and place around wreath. Slip-stitch fabric closed to cover base. Cut 34 leaf shapes from green polka-dotted fabric and 34 leaf shapes from green print fabric. Stitch 17 green polka-dotted leaves and 17 green print leaves. Stuff leaves and stitch closed. Place leaves around the base of the wreath, switching and overlapping print and polka-dotted leaves. Whipstitch the leaves to each other and the base. Stuff twelve 2-inch circles of red polka-dotted fabric with fiberfill to make berries. Tack clusters of berries to the wreath. You may add a red bow for an extra touch.

Greenery Swags

MATERIALS: Assortment of greens; rope; green string; gloves; pruning shears.

INSTRUCTIONS: Begin by soaking the boughs in water overnight. Then, place the rope in the space you want the swag to be. Cut the rope to the appropriate size, leaving extra length at each end for hanging loops. Next, tie the end loops so they can be covered with the greens. After the boughs have been soaked, cut them into 6-inch lengths. Pick an end of the rope to start with and fasten a few stems at a time, facing the same direction, with the string. Continue until the swag is finished. For best results, hang the swag first and spray it daily for longer life.

Christmas Stocking

MATERIALS: Large paper bag; red felt; green felt; needle; red thread; a contrasting embroidery floss; eight bells.

INSTRUCTIONS: Draw an 18-inch-long stocking pattern on the paper bag. Use this pattern to cut out two stockings from the red felt. Cut a heel and a toe shape from the stocking pattern. Use this new pattern to cut two heel and two toes pieces from the green felt. Stitch the heels and toes on one side of each stocking. For the most decorative approach, use running stitches or cross-stitches with a contrasting embroidery floss. Now, sew the two stocking pieces together, right sides facing in, with a ¼-inch seam.

To make a cuff, cut a pattern one-third the length of the stocking with a width ¼ inch less than the width of the top of the stocking. For matched points along the edge of the cuff, allow a seam by folding ¼ inch under on one side. Then, fold the rest of the paper in half, then in half once more. Cut a slanted line along one edge of the folded paper to make a point at the edge of the pattern. Cut a cuff with four points by putting one edge of the pattern on a fold of cloth and cut a second cuff.

Seam together the open edges of the cuff and place one cuff inside the other with the seam sides out. Center bottom points between top points and put together the inside-out cuff and stocking along the top edge. To complete, turn the stocking right side out. For decoration you can add bells to the points and a loop for hanging.

Dolly Chains

MATERIALS: Lightweight typing paper.

INSTRUCTIONS: Fold and cut many sheets of the typing paper in half lengthwise. Make a four-cut accordion pleat by folding a piece in half, then folding the two ends back to meet the first fold, and finally fold the paper in half once more. Leaving the paper folded, draw an outline of half a figure, making sure the figure touches both sides. When unfolded, you will have a chain of four identical figures. Repeat the process using the same pattern or create a new one and string all the chains together.

Rainbow Paper Garlands

MATERIALS: Colored paper; ruler; pencil; scissors; glue.

INSTRUCTIONS: Measure and cut strips of paper ½ by 5 inches. While perfect measurements are not important, the more narrow the strips the more appealing the garland. To create a diamond shape, fold two different-colored strips in half, fold out the ends, and then glue the ends together. For a two-sided figure make four equal folds on a strip, creasing two inner folds to the center and folding back the two outer folds. Repeat the process on another strip of paper and connect the tab-ends to create the shape. For a four-sided, winged figure join the matching ends of two different-colored strips with glue. Once the glue has dried, spread the strips to create an oval. Connect two of these ovals to create a three-dimensional figure by gluing one oval inside of the other, forming a cross.

Create many shapes and connect together to create a colorful garland.

Paper Snowflakes

MATERIALS: Thin white paper; scissors; glue; stapler.

INSTRUCTIONS: Cut the paper to measure 11 by 5 inches. Mark ½-inch intervals down the 11-inch side of the paper. Fold the paper, accordion style, using the marks as a guide. With the paper still folded, staple the center, so the staple is parallel to the 5-inch sides. Make a variety of cuts that match above and below the staple to create a symmetrical snowflake. Open the sides and glue together the ends to form a circle. Tie a loop of string through a notch so the snowflake can be hung.

A VARIATION

MATERIALS: Plain white paper; scissors; waxed paper; iron.

INSTRUCTIONS: Cut paper into a square with sides no smaller than 5 inches. Fold a square in half diagonally forming a triangle. Then, fold the triangle in half making a smaller triangle. Now, fold this triangle into thirds by folding one side to the front and the other to the back. This will leave excess paper at the bottom of a newly formed triangle. Trim the excess paper. Next, cut different shapes along the border of the triangle and unfold it to reveal a snowflake. Place your snowflake between a piece of paper and a piece of waxed paper. Put an additional piece of paper on top of the waxed paper and iron on low heat to melt the wax onto the snowflake. Peel off the waxed paper while it is still warm.

WHERE TO SEND
LETTERS TO SANTA

*T*HERE are many ways for your child to mail a letter to Santa Claus. You can simply address an envelope to "Santa Claus, North Pole" and include the correct return address and postage for a standard first-class letter. These letters are answered, with small gifts, by volunteers working for Operation Santa Claus.

To ensure a response, write to Santa c/o Det. 2, 11th WS, Eilson AFB, Alaska, 99702. Enclose a "reply from Santa" with your child's letter and workers for the Air Force Weather Squadron will send your child a reply from Santa. The letter must be sent before December 10th to receive a response before Christmas.

You can get an authentic North Pole postmark on Santa's letter by sending a blank envelope with postage to Postmaster, Attn: Steve Cornelius, North Pole Branch U.S. Post Office, 325 Santa Claus Lane, North Pole, Alaska, 99705-9998. Before December you can expect a response in about 7 or 8 days.

A VISIT FROM ST. NICHOLAS
by Clement C. Moore

'TWAS the night before Christmas, when all through the house
Not a creature was stirring, not even a mouse;
The stockings were hung by the chimney with care,
In hopes that St. Nicholas soon would be there;
The children were nestled all snug in their beds,
While visions of sugar-plums danced in their heads;
And mamma in her 'kerchief, and I in my cap,
Had just settled down for a long winter's nap,
When out on the lawn there arose such a clatter,
I sprang from the bed to see what was the matter.
Away to the window I flew like a flash,
Tore open the shutters and threw up the sash.
The moon on the breast of the new-fallen snow
Gave the luster of mid-day to objects below,
When, what to my wondering eyes should appear,
But a miniature sleigh, and eight tiny reindeer,
With a little old driver, so lively and quick,
I knew in a moment it must be St. Nick.
More rapid than eagles his coursers they came,

And he whistled, and shouted,
    and called them by name;
Now, Dasher! now, Dancer!
    Now, Prancer and Vixen!
On, Comet! On Cupid!
    On, Donder and Blitzen!
To the top of the porch!
    to the top of the wall!
Now dash away! dash away!
    dash away all!
As dry leaves that before
    the wild hurricane fly,
When they meet with an
    obstacle, mount to the sky,
So up to the house-top the
    coursers they flew,
With the sleigh full of toys, and St. Nicholas too.
And then, in a twinkling, I heard on the roof
The prancing and pawing of each little hoof.
As I drew in my hand, and was turning around,
Down the chimney St. Nicholas came with a bound.
He was dressed all in fur, from his head to his foot,
And his clothes were all tarnished with ashes and soot;
A bundle of toys he had flung on his back,
And he looked like a peddler just opening his pack.
His eyes—how they twinkled! His dimples how merry!
His cheeks were like roses, his nose like a cherry!
His droll little mouth was drawn up like a bow,
And the beard of his chin was as white as the snow;
The stump of a pipe he held tight in his teeth,
And the smoke it encircled his head like a wreath;
He had a broad face and a little round belly,
That shook, when he laughed like a bowlful of jelly.
He was chubby and plump, a right jolly old elf,
And I laughed when I saw him, in spite of myself;

A Visit from St. Nicholas

A wink of his eye and a twist of his head,
Soon gave me to know I had nothing to dread;
He spoke not a word, but went straight to his work,
And filled all the stockings; then turned with a jerk,
And laying his finger aside of his nose,
And giving a nod, up the chimney he rose;
He sprang to his sleigh, to his team gave a whistle,
And away they all flew like the down of a thistle.
But I heard him exclaim, ere he drove out of sight,
"Happy Christmas to all, and to all a good-night!"

Happy New Year